THE BOOK THEY COULDN'T BAN

André Morea

THE BOOK
THEY COULDN'T BAN

The miraculous experiences
of a Bible courier
in Romania

LAKELAND
MARSHALL, MORGAN & SCOTT
116 Baker Street
LONDON WIM 2BB

Copyright © André Morea 1976

First published 1976

ISBN 0 551 00589 0

Printed in Great Britain by
Cox & Wyman Ltd., London, Reading and Fakenham

CONTENTS

PART ONE

Bulgaria

1

The box in the attic

IT WAS one of those late autumn mornings when the sun peers feebly out of a pale sky. As I made my way slowly along a narrow, winding street on the outskirts of Sofia, looking for a particular house, the cold morning air heightened the sense of uneasiness that I felt stirring inside me. I was on my way to meet one of the leaders of the Church in Bulgaria.

I soon realised that the number I was seeking could not be far off, and I began to look more intently at the dirty buildings, with their unkempt gardens and dilapidated fences, that loomed up on my right. I passed a dirty white wall, then came to a garden surrounded by a high wooden fence, at the end of which was a low gateway.

I lifted the latch with a trembling hand, and the gate creaked open. Round the back of the house there was a freshly built veranda; a yellow plate announced that I had found the office I was seeking, and I knocked hesitantly at the door.

No reply. I knocked again, and waited. I peered through the window; there were two desks and a dilapidated typewriter, but otherwise the room was empty.

Disappointed, I was about to leave—but something held me back. I glanced round the garden, and my attention was caught by a wide flight of black wooden steps. Old and decaying, they ran up the side of an ancient building and disappeared into the darkness under the roof. They looked far too rickety to support anyone.

7

The large garden was quite empty. At the windows of the adjacent building not a soul was visible. It looked as if I would have to leave without seeing the man I had come to meet. It was my last day in Bulgaria. Disappointment flooded in: I moved to walk away, but something kept my eyes on the flight of steps. For some reason I desperately wanted to know what lay beyond them. Still undecided, I put my briefcase down on the grass and stood there, feeling lonely, helpless and lost.

'Go up the steps!'

The voice, peaceful and reassuring, had come from behind me. I spun round. Someone—it looked like a woman dressed in white—was looking straight at me, and pointing in the direction of the steps. I gazed, dumbfounded.

'Climb up the steps.'

It was a language I had never heard before, and yet I understood it. Something seemed to take hold of me and propel me across the yard to the steps. I climbed quickly, the woodwork creaking and swaying under my feet, and came eventually to a wide, dark entrance. A feeling of apprehension gripped me. Was it a trap? I glanced uncertainly down to where the woman had been—but there was no one in the garden below, just a strange sensation of calm.

I hesitated again, and again felt myself urged on by unseen hands. As I stepped into the darkness I could just make out on my left the outline of a narrow door with a broken handle. I paused to listen: floorboards creaked on the other side of the door. At last I plucked up the courage to knock quietly. There was no reply; so I knocked again, and this time someone came. I heard a key turn in the lock.

In the dim room I could see the slight form of an old, white-haired lady with sparkling eyes. I blurted out: 'I am a Christian from Romania.'

For a moment she stood stock still, her face registering no reaction. She peered closely at me, as if I were an apparition. Then she motioned to me to come in.

I found myself in a small room, sparsely furnished with

8

a small stove, a rough wood table, an old black bed and a chair. The old lady put her finger to her lips and stared at me so intently that I had to lower my eyes. Her yellow index finger and her narrow lips began to tremble, and tears came into her eyes. Then, suddenly, she came up to me, hugged me, and kissed me on both cheeks. She took me by the shoulders and looked deep into my eyes.

'*Brataa ... brataa ... ia ... davno ... chekaiu ... teba.*'

I did not know Bulgarian, but to my astonishment I could understand the old lady's words. 'Brother,' she had said, 'brother, I have been waiting for you for a long time.' I stood there, not knowing how to reply. Sensing my embarrassment, she reassured me:

'I am M. Sister M.'

Her voice had now become strong and powerful. It was as if an unseen person, greater than her, was speaking through her. I looked at her vacantly, not knowing what to make of it, and she gazed back, wondering why I did not understand. I had never heard her name before. At last she indicated that I should sit down, and I racked my brains for something to say—in any language. There were many things I wanted to know.

Wiping the tears from her eyes, she continued, 'I knew you would come. I was sure of it.' She gazed upwards, and from the way her lips moved and the tears welled up in her eyes I knew that she walked closely with God, and had experienced many answers to prayer.

At last I came down to earth again and began to speak, but she put her finger to her lips.

'No one must hear us,' she warned in a low voice.

'Why have you been waiting for me, of all people?' I asked, almost whispering in her ear. She offered no reply, but continued to watch me closely. Then she crept over to the door, turned the key in the lock – and seemed uncertain what to do next.

At last she plucked up sufficient courage, stooped and took a firm hold of two cords which lay under the bed. With a great effort she dragged out a heavy cardboard box, sealed with tape and a knotted rope, and then slumped back on the bed, exhausted. But she continued to stare at me.

'I was waiting for you to come and collect this,' she said.

I did not know what to think: the whole incident was like a dream. And Sister M kept looking at me to gauge my reactions. At last she took a knife and began carefully to open the box. As she prised open the cardboard flaps with her fingers, a large quantity of gleaming New Testaments came into view. It was like taking the lid off a gold mine—I was dumbfounded. My heart beat fast, and I stood there speechless. For the first time in my life, after twenty years of longing and searching, I was looking at a new New Testament, a new Bible—and in my own language!

The contents of the box seemed to give off the sort of glow you see in some old paintings. I was afraid to touch the gleaming blue mass, for I found it hard to believe that what I had been waiting for for so long was actually here, in front of my eyes. I was soon on my knees, and I saw that Sister M was, too. Both of us began to thank God, each in our own language. How long we remained in prayer I do not know; all I can remember are the deep shadows swimming around in that dingy room, and on each side of the box two dark patches, produced by our tears as we prayed.

Everything seemed so unreal. As I gazed again at the box my head began to swim. Sister M looked at me out of the corner of her eye from time to time, and I could see that she was in a state of ecstasy: her face glowed as if from some secret source of light.

When I eventually came out of my trance, I got up and went over to the box. The blue cover of the New Testament seemed to me to embody all the glories of heaven. As if guided by some unseen hand, I put it to my lips and began to kiss it with all the enthusiasm of a thirsty man drinking at an oasis.

For someone who has grown up with easy access to the Word of God, it is hard to imagine what a profoundly moving experience this was. But it must be good to know that money put in a collection plate in some obscure old church can bear such fruit. I am sure that when we meet in heaven, and all the sacrifices you have made in terms of giving and actually bringing these Bibles to our people are reviewed in the light of eternity, we who have benefited from your kindness will be the first to fall at your feet and thank you—with just as much feeling as I gave thanks to our heavenly Father on that day when I knelt in that small, dilapidated attic in Sofia.

Sister M watched me, smiling. My eyes seemed glued to that New Testament, which I let fall open at the words of the apostle John: 'God is love.' Never had I received such a penetrating and profoundly satisfying revelation of the meaning of those words; they marked themselves indelibly on my soul. I vowed then that for nothing in the world would I give these books up, and I have never gone back on this.

This was without doubt the most wonderful experience of my life. Never again have I felt the same happiness. In many difficult circumstances I have still been comforted by this vision, in lonely nights and in places where I expected least to receive comfort. And it has taught me that the deepest joy is to be found where God has his protecting hand.

'How are you going to take them away?' asked the old lady, coming to the practical details.

'I don't know, but I'll take them,' I replied. It was a problem to which I had not given much thought as yet. Worried, she looked around for something suitable to pack the Bibles in, but could find nothing. So I asked her to fetch me some paper and string to make two packets—one to carry under each arm. She rummaged around under the bed, eventually bringing out some sheets of white paper. I wrapped the books in two packets, secured them with string, then straightened up to see how heavy they were. They were heavy enough. Sister M grew more and more concerned, but I pretended not to notice.

Then she said, 'How are you going to get them across the border?'

I faltered. The very thought made me shudder. 'I don't know . . . but the Lord knows,' I replied.

Sister M looked hard at me, and I gazed rather helplessly up at the ceiling. She motioned to me to kneel down and pray with her. In a halting prayer I placed myself entirely in the hands of the Lord. Only then did I receive the assurance that everything would go well. I shall always remember how I prayed then, the prayer I kept repeating on my journey back to Romania: 'The Word is yours, O Lord. I ask you to watch over it. I am not able, and I have no strength; my hope is in you.'

Both of us were conscious that we were communicating directly with God: I had an inner confirmation of this at the deepest level of soul and spirit. We felt that he was looking down on us, that he was near us, that we were speaking directly to him just as we might speak to the closest of friends.

I shook hands with Sister M.

'I'll be praying for you from now until you go across,' she said.

I climbed warily down from the darkened attic. As I emerged into the light I was completely disorientated by the brightness; yet in my soul I felt a calm joy and wonderful happiness. The earth, the sky all seemed to belong to me—and I, without a shadow of doubt, belonged to God.

2

Frontier crossing

WITH A few hours still before my train was due to leave, I left my luggage at the station and went for a stroll in the town. I wanted to relax and prepare myself for the night frontier crossing. The fresh air was invigorating. I pictured the reactions of fellow-Christians, young and old—the joy on their faces as they received copies of the Word of God. A soft, mysterious warmth invaded all my being.

Gradually, however, my joy began to give way to uneasiness. In my imagination the thankful, happy faces faded, to be replaced by the hard features of the customs officials—packets opened, Bibles spilling out ... police ... interrogations ... The scene faded, only to reappear, this time in different colours, with other sensations, other questions. Little by little, my happiness melted and worries began to crowd back.

Then I seemed to see Sister M again, praying, full of faith and thanksgiving. I saw the old attic, the big box of Bibles and New Testaments. How was I going to get them through the customs? If they were discovered, what would happen to me?

'O Lord,' I cried silently, 'it's your Word, you must protect it. I can't do anything. I'm too weak.' Then almost unconsciously there came into my mind the words of a hymn:

'I will never leave you nor forsake you.'

That is what he has promised me.

Every time these lines came to me, they brought renewed inward assurance. Once again I saw the radiant faces of those to whom I was taking the Bibles; I shared their joy, their excitement, and I fell on my knees with them and thanked the Lord. In a mysterious way God was speaking to me, reassuring me. I did not really understand what was going on: I had had too little experience of God to be able to understand that whenever we go in his name there is no reason for us to be afraid.

Soon after I boarded the train another passenger came into my compartment. He was also a Romanian—an older man, thin, with white hair and a wrinkled face. I helped him to put his suitcase on the luggage rack.

'What's the frontier crossing like?' he asked anxiously.

'It had better be smooth,' I said with an encouraging smile.

'May God grant that,' he mumbled, and sank back into the seat facing me. He was visibly agitated. One minute the motion of the train would lull him off to sleep, the next he would wake up with a jolt, as if someone had shaken him violently.

As we neared the frontier my companion jumped to his feet and took down his suitcase, which he proceeded to unlock. He rearranged the contents nervously, trying all possible permutations. At last, satisfied that he had hit upon the right combination, he turned to me triumphantly.

'I haven't made a bad job of it, have I?'

'No, you shouldn't have any problems.'

'I've heard that the customs officers are very strict. I've been told that they check on the money you have, and if . . . No, I haven't really bought much.' He stopped short, gave me a piercing look and blurted out, 'I do have a leather coat. But nearly everybody brings out one of those. Do you think they will take it from me?'

'I don't expect so,' I reassured him, my gaze shifting instinctively to the two packets on the rack above me.

'You seem very calm,' he commented.

'Why shouldn't I be?'

'I see that you have more luggage than me. What's in those big parcels?'

14

'Bread. White bread.'

'Oh, I see. The customs won't make a fuss about that.' And he sank back into his own thoughts, looking alternately at my packets and his suitcase. Silence descended in the compartment, and again in my mind I could hear the customs officers asking me what I had in my luggage, telling me to open the packets . . . A shiver went down my spine.

For a moment I regretted having brought so many Bibles. Doubts crowded into my mind. Why had I got mixed up in this in the first place? Then I saw again Sister M and heard her thin, sparrow-like voice telling me, 'I prayed that the Lord would send you.' Then a whole host of people, receiving Bibles with tears in their eyes. The promise came to my mind again: 'I will never leave you, nor forsake you.'

I lay down on the seat and tried to get some sleep, but without success. I was infected by the restlessness of my fellow-passenger: fear grew again, until it seemed to throttle me like an iron hand. Trembling, I prayed continuously, 'Lord, please protect your Word. I am powerless and helpless, and count on you . . . I have done all that I can . . . it is up to you to do the rest.'

And I prayed for sleep. The train accelerated down into a valley, and the rhythmic rocking of the carriage, the exhaustion and the strain made my eyelids heavy. Soon a relaxing warmth invaded me. I closed my eyes.

'The customs are coming,' a voice called in the corridor, and I sat up with a jolt. My companion was pacing round like a tiger in a cage.

The train pulled up at a station. Through the frosted window came the first timid rays of early morning sunshine, and there was a hubbub at the end of the carriage. The squeaking and rattling of doors opening and shutting drew nearer. The harsh voices of the customs officers and the noise of their heavy boots echoed along the corridor. I looked at the packets again, and my soul seemed to freeze. My hands began to tremble. What should I do? What should I say?

The old man looked at me in surprise. 'What's the matter? Are you worried about the bread?'

I could not stop trembling. It was too late to turn back. I was trapped, and could only fling myself on the mercy of the Lord. My freedom was at stake; I cried silently again, 'Lord, for the sake of those who are thirsting for your Word, protect these Bibles.'

The door opened abruptly. Two men in grey uniform—Bulgarian customs officers—came in and asked for our customs declarations. They stamped the forms and looked up at the luggage racks.

'What have you bought in our country?' my companion was asked.

'Just a few presents.'

The officer helped him down with his case and went through his things. His colleague looked at me for a while and then stared vacantly out of the window, apparently contemplating something in the distance. The silence was broken only by the rustle of clothes as the old man's case was searched. The second officer sat down beside me, but continued to look out of the window. Still tense, I did the same.

The sound of the case snapping shut made me jump. The second officer shifted his gaze from the window and stood up.

'Let's go.'

'Have a good journey,' said the other, and shut the door noisily behind him.

The old man was breathing more freely, and I began to feel much more at ease. Already I could picture myself distributing Bibles in distant villages. Everything within me welled up in praise to God.

'They didn't even look in your stuff, did they?' the old man suddenly recalled. 'Fantastic! Perhaps they realised you only had bread.'

Further up the carriage, more sounds—doors being opened and closed, the clatter of boots and the sound of raised voices.

'The Romanians,' he said, eyeing his suitcase. I was brought up with a jolt. He tried to reassure himself: 'If the Bulgarians didn't ask me anything, why should the Romanians?' A pause. 'On the other hand, I've heard the Romanians are worse . . .'

I said nothing, but I began to tremble again as I heard the Romanians approaching. I looked at the packets, knowing that nothing escaped the eagle eyes of my fellow-countrymen. The Bulgarians would only have confiscated the books, but the Romanians . . . They would call the police, there would be interrogations, trouble at work, a trial, sentence . . . I saw them opening the packets, myself frozen with horror. My stomach contracted. I was shaking like a leaf. Then from somewhere within me, those words: 'I will never leave you, nor forsake you.'

A rattling sound, and the door was flung open. Two young customs officials stepped into the compartment and looked up at the racks, estimating how much work they had to get through. The lean one with long side-boards turned to my neighbour. While he was rummaging around in his luggage and haggling about duty on the leather jacket, his colleague turned to me.

'Is this hold-all all you have?'

'As you can see,' I replied casually, opening the bag. My heart was pounding, and I broke out in a cold sweat.

'No thanks; that won't be necessary,' he said, and glanced up at the rack. An iron hand seemed to grab me. What was I going to do? I imagined the packets being opened and froze. I went completely numb.

'If only every passenger just had a hold-all, a customs officer's life would be a lot easier.' He looked at the rack again, as if to make sure that his eyes weren't playing tricks. 'There you are—the model tourist!' he said with a yawn, then turned to his colleague. 'I've finished. This fellow is really travelling light.'

'I'm through as well,' said the other. 'Have a pleasant journey,' he added in our direction as they left the compartment.

A terrible limpness came over me. The carriage seemed to be swimming before my eyes, and I was struck dumb. Then, little by little, I recovered and, gripping the edge of the seat to steady myself, I felt a wave of warmth engulf me. The tightness in my throat relaxed, and tears flowed down my cheeks. I was going through an experience impossible to describe. Everything within me cried out, 'The Lord has saved me.' At last I understood the full impact of those words, 'I will never leave you nor forsake you.' I reproached myself for lack of faith in his promises.

I felt like hugging and kissing the old man opposite me; I wanted to cry, to rejoice, to go round telling everyone what a miracle God had done for me. But the train was still standing in the station, and no one seemed to be moving. Doubts assailed me again. What if the men came back? Perhaps, suspecting the contents of the packets, they had thought it best to go and consult with their chief . . .

I went out into the corridor and looked out of the window. The customs officers were leaving the train, escorting some men and women carrying opened luggage. The early sun bathed everything in a soft glow. The engine gave a short, sharp whistle, and the train began to move again, leaving the station, and its customs officers, far behind.

And I had the conviction, which to this day has not left me, that all the time Sister M had been praying in her little room—that as the first rays of dawn began to strike the attic window she rose from her knees with great joy, thanking the Lord for the wonderful victory he had granted.

I stood at the open window, letting the wind cool my flushed cheeks.

3

'We want Bibles!'

ON A MAP of Romania I had underlined in red the places where Christians were to be found. I tried to recollect where the greatest need was, to decide where the Word of God should go first. Beside me were the two packets of Bibles. How small they seemed. If only I could have had ten such packets, I thought, looking at the mass of red on the map. Churches in nearly every area, and Christians everywhere, needed Bibles. What were a hundred books among thousands of churches and tens of thousands of believers?

I sighed. If only I had the opportunity to bring in enough Bibles to meet all needs. I prayed hard and long, racking my brains for a plan. But the more I thought about it, the more my feeling of helpless failure grew. I felt utterly crushed. I cried out, 'Lord, I don't know the answer, but I am at your disposal. No matter where you send me, I will go and take your Word.'

Then I experienced peace, but I was still unable to come to a decision. I had only a certain number of Bibles, and no chance of obtaining more. And there was no way that I could see of sharing out those I had on any kind of equal basis. So I prayed, 'Show me which way I should go. Let each copy find its way to where there is the greatest need.'

As I prayed I began to experience a strange, melting sensation. I seemed to be evaporating—dissolving and somehow becoming submerged in nothingness, while my eyes opened—to reveal a vision.

Terrified, I looked around me. I was standing on a large rock, on the brink of a precipice. Hundreds of people were climbing up towards me—children, men and women, young and old, dressed in gaily coloured clothes.

They were climbing with difficulty, and making a lot of noise. Some seemed to be calling out.

The crowd was getting nearer, and had begun coming up the rock on all sides. I stood there, completely cut off, on an island. I could not understand what was going on, and started to panic. Then I heard a sound in the distance like a horn, entreating but commanding: 'Bi ... bles, Bi ... bles'. And the whole crowd kept on coming towards me, climbing and calling out for the Word of God.

A shudder passed through me. The crowd became menacing; they were after something I did not have. Where could I get enough Bibles? I had spent twenty years looking for one for myself.

Still the people kept coming, and by now they were climbing over the top. The nearer they came, the clearer I could hear what they were shouting, and I felt smaller and smaller. They would soon be crushing me, flattening me and squashing me. For a moment my eyes turned back to look at myself and saw a tiny man, small as a doll. Then, from what seemed to be a bluish cloud, just above my head, I heard a voice.

'You need do nothing else.'

Like an echo, bounced between two mountains, the words went on and on ...

As the crowd came even closer, I could make out faces I knew. I searched for something to say, but they began to make a circle round me, and from the centre of the throng a man whose face seemed familiar—but who was of enormous stature—stepped out and demanded, 'We want Bibles.'

Then all the crowd, as one person, stretched out their hands towards me. I stood rooted to the spot, trembling, not knowing what to say. Where could I get all those Bibles?

The vision faded, and I found myself back in my room, with head still bowed, in a cold, hostile atmosphere. My eyes were full of tears, and I was shaking all over.

As I stood up my eyes, still dim, fell on the map, on the northern part of the country—and I took it as a sign. Drying my eyes, I slumped into a chair, my thoughts still on my vision. There was pain in my chest, and I felt completely helpless. The more I thought about it, the less I could see a solution to the problem. Why had I been chosen for this job? I still ask myself the same question.

The vision obsessed me to the point of torture. There were not many Bibles, and my free time was very limited. At last, though, I got time off from work, packed a suit-case full of Bibles and hurried for the northbound train. I only just caught it, and had to stand in the crowded cor-ridor, my face glued to the window, watching the trees, villages and telegraph poles flit by.

The vision remained with me; I could see the crowds straining for Bibles. A shiver went down my spine. I looked at the suitcase. I knew now where I was going to distribute those Bibles, but they were just a drop in the bucket . . .

My feet were beginning to ache, and at the first stop I managed to obtain a corner seat. I sensed that the Lord was with me, and that he was caring for me in my tired-ness; as I meditated on this a mysterious warmth filled me in spite of the fatigue. That night I would be in the company of Christians.

Sitting next to me was a man with a coarse peasant's coat and ruddy complexion. He looked sharply at me, then let his gaze wander round the carriage and finally out of the window. Perhaps he knew the hymn tune I was humming? Might he be a fellow-believer?

A tall lady was preparing to leave. I helped her down with her suitcase, and she thanked me.

'Where are we?' asked a man standing in the corridor. But the shutting of the compartment door drowned his question, which was left unanswered.

'It's a town,' interjected a red-faced lady.

'How time flies,' murmured the old man in the peasant's coat.

'And so does our life,' I volunteered suddenly.

He looked at me again, puzzled. His large grey eyes had a strange luminosity. Next to him a slim, middle aged man in a white shirt had seemed to be deep in thought. Now he looked up and, opening his tired eyes, gazed at me searchingly. I pretended not to notice and went on talking to my immediate neighbour.

'Let me see, how old are you? About sixty-five ... sixty-eight?'

'About that,' he replied. 'Difficult years, full of misfortune.'

The man in the white shirt shifted his melancholy gaze from the old man to me and back again. The old man went on, 'What is our life here on earth but a short journey, full of difficulty and worry? I've been through two wars. Look here,' (he rolled up his sleeve), 'I've got a shell splinter to prove it.'

'You've been lucky,' his wife interrupted. She was plump, red-cheeked, with a wide mouth, and wore her hair in a large bun. 'The Lord has protected you. He does not want wars; he is a God of peace.'

At that moment I looked across at the slim man, who was still pretending to be preoccupied with his own thoughts. He looked up and out of the window, but I could see he was listening closely.

'Yes, that's right,' said the old man. 'I never used to go into battle without making the sign of the cross and kissing my little icon of the virgin Mary.'

'Look,' I told him, 'an icon cannot help you; nor can the sign of the cross. Only God, Jesus the Saviour, can, because he loves you and wants to give you eternal life.'

'That could be so, Ernest,' said his wife. 'You have had so much luck. The gentleman is right. Perhaps you ought to become a monk.'

'In the trenches,' said the old man thoughtfully, 'there was a young man they called Holy Joe. He never used to leave the trench for an attack without reading from a book with a black leather cover which he called the Word of God. I never had time to get into conversation with him—he was soon transferred. He was a good-natured fellow, though. Survived the war, too. I met him not long ago.'

'The Lord protects his children,' I replied. 'He has allowed you to live this long so that you can hear the Word of God and become a child of his.'

'A child of God? What is that?' the old man asked.

The man in the white shirt kept looking curiously at me. There was something suspicious about him. But, I said to myself, whoever he is, he must hear the Word of God, about the sacrificial death of Jesus Christ ... I would probably never meet him again ... I had to witness for the Lord Jesus Christ and about his salvation.

'Many people that you meet today,' I said, 'may call themselves Christians and even make the sign of the cross. They may have been going to church for years, but still they turn round and blaspheme and insult Christ and the Church. We say that if a man says he is a Christian, he must prove it by his life.'

'That's right,' mumbled the wife, looking out of the window.

'The man you mentioned was like that, and you admired him. Why don't you repent—you and ...' I hesitated for a moment '... the gentleman over there—because everyone has sinned.'

'No, I wouldn't say that,' said the old man, rather embarrassed.

'What are you afraid of?' I asked. 'Haven't you sinned?'

'Aha,' he said nervously, 'many times.'

'Well then, confess your sins to God, resolve to break with the old sins and live a holy life—that is what repentance is. Are you ashamed to tell God that you have sinned against him? Jesus knows about everything you have ever done anyway; so you might as well tell him!'

'No—o,' murmured the old man.

'That's what we'll do,' said his wife.

'Jesus Christ died on the cross to cleanse you from all sins, however bad they may be and however many you have committed. Then, once you are washed, cleansed and your sins are forgiven and forgotten, you become a new man—you become a child of God.'

'Where did you get all this from?' interrupted the man in the white shirt.

I gave him a straightforward answer, and he was quite

23

astounded. 'Have you studied dialectical materialism?' he asked.

'Of course—it's very interesting,' I replied. 'In fact it was scientific materialism that led me to God.' The man raised his eyebrows in astonishment.

'Just as it is proper to confess one's sins,' I went on, addressing the old man, 'so it is just as proper to bind oneself not to sin any more. It is a form of commitment.' I used a term common in political meetings, and the man in the white shirt smiled discreetly, giving me courage to go on. After all, I had never heard of any law that forbade such discussions on trains.

'Oh dear,' sighed the old man, 'our Orthodox Church is not what it used to be.'

I looked him in the eye. 'Neither the Church nor religion can save a man's soul. Neither indulgences nor almsgiving can forgive your sins—only Jesus Christ, through his blood shed on the cross, can save you.'

'What about me?' asked the man in the white shirt sardonically.

'You too, because you have sinned, and because you also want to find eternal happiness,' I replied. His expression changed, and he looked more serious. His smile disappeared, and he fell into deep thought.

'All men without exception need to come to Jesus Christ, because all without exception have sinned against him,' I said.

'You could be right,' said the slim man quietly.

Silence descended once again in the compartment. Everyone seemed plunged deep in thought, but the man in the white shirt still kept looking at me. He struck me as being a good man. I did not imagine that I would have any problems.

'Are you getting off at the next station?' he asked.

'Yes,' I replied. He could turn me in, of course. It was always a possibility.

'Good,' he remarked laconically. And once again the conversation lapsed.

The conductor, looking faintly ridiculous in a hat too

small for his head, came down the corridor, calling out the name of the next station. I took down my suitcase and began to edge towards the door. After me came the man in the white shirt.

On the platform I was borne along by a wave of struggling passengers. I made for the exit, hoping to escape the notice of the man in the white shirt. But he, not having so much to carry, managed to reach the exit just as I did.

Outside the station he came up behind me as I paused for breath and said: 'Congratulations. I like a man who knows what he wants. Justice is on your side—and probably also truth.'

I looked at him astonished, not knowing what to say. He stared at me hard for a few seconds, glanced hastily this way and that and then turned towards me again.

'I am a captain in the secret police. I can guess where you are going, and I probably know what your name is. As far as I am concerned, you are free to go.'

'Thank you,' I mumbled.

'But no one must know of our meeting. Is that understood?' Before I could reply, he made off at high speed. I stood there dumfounded; his disclosure had taken my breath away completely. I made a quick decision. I would leave the place as soon as I could.

A biting wind seemed to cut right through me, and back at the station I was shivering with cold. Once again, I only just caught the train I wanted.

Three stops back I got off at a small, empty station. It was freezing cold outside, but inside I felt as if I had just emerged from a fiery furnace.

4

Receiving the Word with joy

FOR A FEW moments I stood in the station entrance, unable to get my bearings. Then I remembered; I had to go round the station and take the first street on the left. I walked with difficulty, shifting the suitcase constantly from one hand to the other. I no longer felt the cold. Joyfully I contemplated the prospect of being with fellow-believers again, and quickened my pace.

The streets were dark and empty. After a while the houses seemed unfamiliar, and I came to a halt. I had lost my bearings. My mind went a complete blank. I stood there as the wind rattled the branches of the trees, and began to wonder if I should retrace my steps. Then a stronger gust brought a new sound in the night—the whispered lines of a hymn.

For a moment I thought my ears were playing tricks on me, but the meeting was there, just along the street. I reached a small house, typical of the region, surrounded by a high fence into which was built a covered gateway of old boards with a dilapidated roof. The strains of the hymn were coming from a dimly lit window. As I approached I could make out the words, 'Nearer, my God, to thee'.

I eased my way in just as they were kneeling to pray; so I put my suitcase under the bench and knelt with them. The room was full, and the warmth quickly penetrated. Soon my cheeks were glowing like torches. As I prayed I kept asking the Lord who I should give the Bibles to first. I asked him to show me those in greatest need – for none of them, so far as I could see, had a Bible. 'Lord,' I prayed, 'let the one to whom I should give your Word be the first to come towards me and invite me home.'

The prayers went on for a long time, followed by two

more hymns. Then a brother who had recognised me came up and invited me to speak to the congregation. During the last verse of the hymn I made my way to the front.

On the table used as a pulpit there was an old Bible, very worn, its pages yellow with age. The whole of Genesis was missing, and so was the first part of Exodus, together with a large part of Revelation. The ink of the many underlinings had run, so that it was often hard to read the original text. The corners and edges of the pages were badly worn. The cover, which was stuck with paste to the binding, was in tatters, and had obviously once belonged to another book.

I announced my text and looked up. Only one man in the whole room had a Bible, in which he was trying feverishly to find the text. A shiver went down my spine. As I stood there facing that great number of people, I seemed to recognise in them the same crowd that had surged towards me in my vision, their hands outstretched for the Word of God.

No one seemed anxious to leave after the message, but little by little they began to drift away. What would happen now, I wondered, if I stood up and offered Bibles to anyone who wanted them? I pictured them falling over each other as they rushed towards me. Then I remembered that even among the first disciples there had been a Judas, and I waited.

Soon someone came towards me. He was a short, middle-aged man with brown hair, and he was poorly dressed. I noticed his drawn face and deep-set eyes as he made his way cautiously in my direction. He seemed to want to say something, but could not pluck up the courage to say it. I stretched out my hands to him.

'Brother,' he said quietly, a note of apology and pleading in his voice, 'the Lord has told me to invite you to our house. I am poor, and haven't much of the things of this world, though I do have a lot of children, but I am grateful to the Lord for all that I do have. Come to our house. You can see what the Lord gives us.'

I found his reserve very touching, but before I could

say a word he had picked up my suitcase and I was following him towards the door. Before we reached it another brother, who had been looking on, came quickly up to me and whispered in my ear:

'This brother of ours is very kind-hearted, but very poor. He has many mouths to feed and can hardly make ends meet. You will find it very hard to sleep there. There's hardly any space.'

I was in a quandary. I didn't want to be a burden to the first man, and yet I saw him as an answer to prayer. In an effort to compromise, I asked, 'Do you two live near each other?'

'Only a few doors away,' they replied together.

So I agreed to have supper at the first man's house, and to spend the night with the other.

We left the church and found ourselves on a narrow street. It was beginning to snow. The cold cut into me again, but it was not long before we reached the first house. Ducking our heads, we entered a dark hallway with an earthen floor. On the right, someone heard us and opened a door, weak light filtering through the opening. We went into a large room, in the middle of which stood a large table with a lamp on it. Spaced along the walls were beds of bare boards, arranged in an open-ended square; they also served as seats for the table. There were only two actual chairs to be seen, near the door. On the wall to the right hung an old framed text, 'As for me and my house, we will serve the Lord'. In a corner fire glowed in an old stove. All the walls were scratched, and in places covered with graffiti.

A short, plump woman was busying herself with the bedcovers. She looked at me shyly but welcomingly and invited me to sit down in one of the two chairs near the door, next to a small child in a cot. I had hardly sat down when I heard the clatter of many feet. The door burst open, and a noisy crowd of children rushed in. I counted them. There were ten.

'There are two more who are not here,' said their mother.

'Children,' said their father confidentially, 'take off

your coats and come and kneel down with us. Thank the Lord that he has brought us a guest this evening.'

Like a chorus of tiny birds they raised their little voices in a prayer of thanksgiving to God. When we rose from our knees an old man with white hair fringing a shining bald pate was standing near the door.

'This is my father,' said the host. The old man was dressed in a long linen blouse-like garment which came down to below his waist, where it was held in place by a faded red sash. His cheeks sagged above a long white beard and his eyes were half-hidden beneath two bushy, snow-white eyebrows.

'How old are you, brother?' I asked.

'Just turned eighty.'

'Praise the Lord! I can see that you are still as youthful as an eagle.'

'He can read without glasses!' called out one of the children.

'Really?' I said. 'Let's give you a reading test.'

'Why not?' said the old man benignly.

I put down my suitcase and, opening it carefully, drew out one of the bigger Bibles, with a black cover and beautiful red edging. The family looked at me spell-bound.

'Read this, brother. This print should suit you,' I said, trying hard to restrain a smile.

The old man gripped the book in trembling hands. He looked at the front and the back, and at the gold lettering on the spine, stroked the red edging of the pages and then read from the cover. 'Bi ... ble,' he said, very slowly, 'or Ho ... ly Scrip ... ture of the Old and New Testaments ... with footnotes.' Then, moistening his finger, he turned the first page. 'In the beginning God created the heaven and the earth.' Looking up, he beamed with happiness.

'What a treasure you have, brother. What a treasure.' And my host, too, put out his hand and began to stroke the cover, feeling the grain of the cloth.

'That's wonderful workmanship, brother. If only we had one in the house, with all these children ...'

By this time the children had gathered round and were

gazing at the Bible as if it were some miraculous object that had fallen straight from heaven. Each child strained forward to get a better look, and to touch it. Only the mother stood aside, watching.

'Brother,' I said slowly, 'God has sent me here to bring you this Bible.'

'What?' The old man did not know what to believe.

'The Lord has sent me to bring you this Bible.'

He looked at me, wiped the tears from his eyes and pressed the Bible to his chest. His old and wrinkled hands began to tremble, and his beard quivered. Two tears started down his yellow cheeks.

'I thought I was going to be with the Lord without ever having seen a Bible in this house,' he said, and fell on his knees. 'I thank you Lord that you have heard the prayer that I prayed every day, and that you have not allowed my eyes to close in death without having seen your Word in this home.' Then we all knelt and thanked the Lord together, tears of joy filling our eyes.

It was very late when we set out for the place where I was to spend the night. There were only a few yards to go, but the cold was already cutting through me when we reached a modest house with light streaming from its large windows. Hearing our steps, the householder came to meet us at the door. They had been waiting for me.

According to the custom among believers in that part of the country, we immediately knelt to thank the Lord for allowing us to come together. I had discovered the truth, which I had been slow to learn, that true happiness is only to be found as we give ourselves fully to the Lord's work and are engaged in the service of others.

We sat down, and my former host remained with us. There was such a warmth of fellowship; all the faces were serene and bright. But this serenity did not come from outward calm, as my new host quickly revealed.

'Not far from here, to the north,' he told me, 'some of our brothers wanted to enlarge their meeting room; so they knocked down one of the partition walls. For this they were fined—many times.'

'Yes,' sighed the other, 'and they have begun to put us under observation.' He paused, then went on, 'It is in Bistrita. Many are turning to the Lord there, and the room where they meet can no longer hold them all. They are packed in like sardines. So they thought it would be a good idea to knock out the inside wall. They did, but there was a Judas among them . . .

'It was denounced as political by the head of the People's Council—or whatever he's called—and they received a note saying they had contravened article I-don't-know-what of a law that I don't believe even exists, and were to be fined 5,000 lei.'

'Five thousand!' exclaimed our host in surprise.

'Yes—one man's wages for a month. They made an appeal. They did everything possible.

' "In vain—all in vain, brother," they told me. "We are never in the right. So we paid. What else could we do? And we went on paying, over and over again. Five times they gave us the same fine for the same wall." '

'And what did the appeal court do?' I asked.

'Oh, the appeal court. The judge just opened the file on the case and read out, "We rule that the fine is still valid—5,000 lei." '

'How much longer will God put up with such a system?' sighed my host.

'Do you know,' the other man went on, 'the church president, Bochian, came and told them to put up the wall again. He said they ought to submit to the authorities. When a brother told him that that was not how he understood the Word of God, the president went red in the face and shouted at him, "You are always trying to make things difficult for me. Unless you put that wall back, I shall excommunicate you." '

There was a long silence. The atmosphere, which had become unbearably tense, was lifted only by a final moment of prayer.

Then my first host returned home, his face shining with joy and happiness. I could imagine him going straight to his new Bible when he got in the door.

'I have waited a long time to speak to someone about

31

the Word of God,' said my new host, when we were left alone. 'There are so many problems. I would be very glad if you would tell me what you think about ... But perhaps you'd like a rest first?' He hesitated.

'While it is day we must work,' I said. 'The night is coming, when no one can work. Let's use the time.'

He faltered again. 'Oh dear. I've forgotten to bring the Bible from the church, and I don't own one.'

'Don't worry,' I said; 'take mine.' He heaved a sigh of relief. His wife and children were in the other room, preparing for bed. I could see that he was agitated by many problems. I took out a Bible and handed it to him. He took it, looked at it, turned it over, flicked over the pages.

'How beautiful it is!'

'The Word of God is beautiful wherever it is found,' I said.

'Where can I get a Bible like this, brother? For ten years I have been looking for a Bible, and during all that time I have been asking the Lord to send me his Word. I have never given up hope. Perhaps I am not worthy enough. Not long ago I heard someone had managed to buy a Bible—I don't know where—for 600 lei. That's very, very expensive, but it is the Word of God, and worth any price.'

'I know. Keep praying to God, and somehow you will get a Bible from somewhere. Only he can do it.'

'Yes, brother, we do pray without ceasing. Did you see how many people there were at the meeting? Not one of them has a Bible, and yet they all pray for one.'

'I am absolutely convinced that the Lord hears the prayers of his saints,' I said.

'So am I,' he responded quickly.

'I believe that it will not be long before your prayers are answered.'

'May the Lord bless you, brother, for your faith.' He turned the Bible over in his hands, stroking it, just like a child with a new toy. I tried to imagine what his reaction would be when he realised I was going to give it to him.

Half jokingly, I told him: 'I can see that you need a Bible; so I'll give you this one and find myself another. In the big towns, you know, it's quite easy.'

He looked at me for a long time and then lowered his gaze—but he did not say anything.

'You did say you needed one, didn't you?' I prompted.

He turned over the pages of the book. Something seemed to be troubling him. 'I'm not ready,' he said slowly. 'I haven't enough money. I earn only a small amount, and I have so many expenses.'

I felt an inward tension. I thought of the Bible, and of all the other people in the area who needed one. There must be a great many.

'I received this Bible from the Lord,' I said, 'and in his name I give it to you.'

He shivered and gave me a rather scared look. He closed the Bible, looked at it again, then stared at me. His lips were trembling slightly. 'Brother,' he burst out suddenly, 'I'm not worthy of such a gift.' And he placed both hands on the Bible, stroking it lightly as if he were afraid it might explode. All the time his gaze was lowered, and he seemed to be preoccupied with other thoughts. Two large tears rolled down his cheeks.

'Lord Jesus,' he sobbed. 'You have heard my prayers. You have seen my need. You knew my thirst. Oh, how I thank you. Help me to make you known everywhere.'

And instead of scrutinising the Word as we had intended, debating various problems, we fell on our knees and thanked the Lord in a long and ardent prayer. As the next day dawned we were still on our knees. The rays of the rising sun filtered through the folds of the yellow curtains, enveloping everything in a diffuse, dancing sheen of light.

During that night, more than at any other time in my experience, we had tasted the pains and also the sweetness of an all-night prayer meeting, in which all our being was taken up by the glory and wonder of God. It was then that we became aware that it is only in prayer, in communion with God, that the Christian can leave the world of time and space behind, to be caught up with God and speak face to face with him.

I felt that my work in that particular place was finished. With my host's agreement we left later that morning for an area not far off, where I knew there was an even greater need of Bibles. We had already heard many things about the Christians there, and we were eager to get to know them.

As the sun climbed in the sky its rays seemed to bite into the cold morning air as sharply as the snow crunched under our feet. I wrapped my overcoat more tightly around me. We had quite a long way to go; so I quickened my pace, and that warmed me up. But the cold air and frost stung my cheeks.

At last we approached the village, and my companion told me, 'The Christians here have for some years been trying to get a small house built where they can worship the Lord, but everyone is against them. Representatives of the official church have stopped them. So they can't come together to worship, because no one will give them permission. Nor have they hope of getting it. The authorities find all sorts of excuses.'

'I don't suppose it stopped there?' I prompted.

'No. You can trust the authorities to be true to type. They also issued a decree forbidding them to invite any Christians from outside to hold meetings, or to allow anyone to preach without official permission.' Such restrictions were not new to me, but these seemed to be particularly severe.

Soon we were walking along a narrow street, past a broken-down fence. The snow which had fallen during the night was still undisturbed. A dog barked somewhere in the distance. Everything else seemed to be asleep.

'Not much further,' said my companion, noticing that I was tired. At the corner of a little lane he pushed open a small gate, through which I followed him into a farmyard which was guarded by two poplar trees. There was a brilliant layer of white on the ground, marked only by a single row of bootprints.

'Someone more hardworking than us has been here,' he said, a little anxiously.

A child in a thin shirt opened the door into a narrow hallway, and we found ourselves in front of another door. My friend knocked and turned the handle, and we saw two men sitting at a low table, engaged in a heated discussion. One of them had a Bible open in front of him, at which he was pointing excitedly. He was a thick-set man, and on his shoulders there were still some traces of snow. The other man, who had a drawn, pallid face and a vacant look, was on the point of taking some papers out of his pocket. He stuffed them hastily back when we entered. It was obvious that they found the interruption embarrassing, but the householder received us amiably and invited us to sit down with the two men.

The discussion started up again, as if we were not there. The tall, thick-set man was saying, 'So you believe, brother, that Jesus Christ heals men today?'

'I do, just as it says in the Word. He is the same yesterday, today and forever,' replied the other quietly. His colourless face seemed like wax.

'Do you believe that the Lord Jesus Christ can heal you too?'

'Yes, I do,' he said, visibly moved.

'But do you believe he can heal you personally?'

'Of course. Why not?' he mumbled.

'Do you believe, Brother G, that Jesus the Saviour can heal you now?'

'Yes,' replied the sick man firmly.

Looking him in the eye, the tall man took the pieces of paper, tore them up and threw them down on the table. 'Let us get down on our knees,' he said.

Everyone in the room knelt down around the table, on which lay the open Bible and the torn up doctors' prescriptions—for medicine for a chronic lung complaint.

I have always believed that God does heal sick people who come to him with all their pain and helplessness—who fall at the foot of the Cross seeking healing. In spite of this I was seized with a deep curiosity, perhaps because I found the proceedings rather strange, and because I had yet to see what I believed actually happen. So as we got down on our knees, I too prayed for this pale brother ravaged by illness, about whom I had heard the previous night.

The thick-set man cleared his throat and, putting his right hand on the forehead of the sick man, began in a solemn voice, full of authority and conviction, 'I thank you, Lord, that you will still heal all our sicknesses and all our infirmities. Your promise is that if we ask anything in your name you will grant it. And so I command you, sickness, suffering, pain or whatever you are—in the name of the Lord Jesus, leave the body of this brother.'

His final words were like a thunderclap; everything in the room was shaken. It was a command which everything and everyone had no choice but to obey. He continued, 'We thank you, our Saviour, that you have healed this child of yours, and we give you all the praise, glory and worship.'

We rose from our knees. The sick man's face was wet with tears and perspiration, but his complexion had now taken on a rosy colour. His eyes, too, were shining. He stood up, dumbfounded, not knowing, it seemed, what was happening to him. He wiped his brow as if he had just woken, straightened up and stretched his arms. He stood motionless for a while, looking at the open Bible and the torn up pieces of paper. Then he broke into a fit of uncontrollable weeping, like a child, rushed towards his friend and embraced him.

It was a very moving scene of elation and deep gratitude to God. No one moved, and no one said a word.

Suddenly I realised the thick-set man had gone. I looked out of the window. Snowflakes were falling, catching the rays of the winter sun. The man had left a trail of glistening footprints behind him.

A short while afterwards, Brother G left as well, overwhelmed with the joy of the Lord—a joy that filled his entire being. His eyes, cheeks and brow all seemed aglow with mysterious radiance—and health.

We were also in a hurry to leave, but I knew that in that house there was no Bible. I looked round, trying to think of somewhere to put one where it would be found easily. Eventually, I managed to slip a Bible under the bedcover.

As we climbed the hill towards the next village, I was engrossed in thought. Then I heard shouting in the distance, and turned to see a figure coming towards us, holding something wrapped in a towel.

'Brothers,' he called out as he drew near, 'someone has left something behind on my bed.' He lowered his voice as he approached. 'A Bible—a beautiful new Bible,' he said, looking at each of us in turn.

'I have mine here,' said my companion.

'So have I,' I said.

He looked at us, puzzled. His eyes wandered from me to my companion and back again.

'Every good and perfect gift comes from the Father of light,' said my companion. 'Thank the Lord for it. Try not to let the dust collect on it, and all will go well for you.'

'Brothers, the Lord has heard my prayers, and that is something to get excited about. Last night I dreamed that I was going along a path in the snow when I found a brand new Bible, just like this one.'

He followed us for a while, his towel-wrapped Bible grasped firmly in his hand.

5

Visited by angels?

SEVERAL YEARS later, after I had come to the West, I was sitting at my desk working on the manuscript of this book, when I was called to the telephone. At the other end was a man who seemed to be trying to speak several languages at once. He said he would like to see me.

I had met him only once before, and that had been many years ago, but his face had stuck in my memory, and I was able to recognise him at the station. As I got off the train he rushed towards me, holding on to the black briefcase that seemed an inseparable part of him. He stopped short, eyed me carefully over the dark glasses which, as usual, had slid down his nose, smiled discreetly and threw his arms round me, slapping me heartily on the back.

It was a Sunday morning, and we went directly to church. He could not stop talking. I gathered he had a number of problems, but began to wonder whether the problems just happened to come his way or whether he was a bit of a problem himself. Words flowed from him like a torrent. He hardly paused for breath, and I could not get a word in edgeways.

After the service he suggested we should go for a short walk. He looked very tired, and his attention kept wandering. We went into the first restaurant we came to.

'It has been so good to see you,' he said as we sat down. He didn't seem to have changed. Still the same pensive, domed forehead, the same silvery grey hair, cut in the same style.

'I can see you haven't changed at all,' I said. 'You are still the same man—eternally youthful.'

The atmosphere was very relaxed. Little by little the conversation worked its way round to the subject of Bulgaria. I was anxious to hear the latest news, particularly regarding my friends there. As my friend was a Bulgarian himself I knew that he must have news to pass on, but I was sorry to hear that it was all bad; the Christians there were being persecuted and having great difficulties. Then he suddenly remembered something.

'It was in autumn 1967,' he said. 'September or October. I was still in Bulgaria at the time. It was one of those beautiful, calm evenings. Sister S, for no particular reason, had opened her window and looked out on to the street, just as two girls came round the corner, each carrying a large parcel. From time to time they stopped and looked round.

' "What are those girls carrying?" she thought. "Whatever it is, it is very heavy." So she ran downstairs to help them. They had just put their parcel down outside the gate to get their breath back.

'Sister S was wondering what she should say to them when they came towards her and slipped past into the courtyard without speaking. She stood there, rooted to the spot. The girls went on a bit further, stopped and put their parcels down, and the taller of the two came towards her, taking out a scrap of paper with an address on it.

'Sister S looked at it. It was her own address.

' "These are for Brother X," said both the girls together, pointing to the parcels.

'Sister S did not know their language, but she understood their meaning. She made signs to the effect that they should come in and have something to eat, rest and spend the night there. Without waiting for a reply she started up the stairs, carrying one parcel. But when she looked down again they were both gone: the one large parcel of books was standing in an otherwise empty courtyard.'

He stopped, raised his eyes and stared fixedly at me. His eyes glistened with tears.

'Perhaps they were angels,' I suggested.

'Neither I nor Sister S knew,' he said, 'but they looked like two ordinary girls—two young people full of energy.'

I saw that he had more to tell me; so I let him take up the threads of the story.

'Two days later, when I was visiting this sister S, I started to undo the packets, because I knew they must contain Bibles or New Testaments. But when I saw they were in Romanian I grew very sad. "Why, Lord? Why send us Romanian Bibles when we need Bulgarian ones? Surely you know we're Bulgarians? What can we do with them?"

'I did nothing but complain, brother. Lord, forgive me. I didn't understand his plan. I didn't know how to wait in patience . . .'

He took his glasses off and dabbed his eyes with his handkerchief.

'It is a wonderful thing to be able to understand God and the way he works, right from the beginning. Or, when we do not understand, to wait in patience, to see what his will is, not to hurry, not to fret.' He coughed, and I saw that tears were coming to his eyes again. Then he recovered his composure.

'As I was saying, when I saw they were in Romanian, and there were so many of them, I didn't know what to do. But one day, when I was alone in prayer in my room, I seemed to hear a voice, whispering in my ear that I should take the books to Sister M in her attic. This thought refused to leave me, and the next day I took the train to Sofia. By nightfall I reached her house.

'When she saw the two parcels she was very surprised. "Bibles," I whispered, putting my finger to my lips. She helped me to bring them in, and after I had sat down and recovered my breath, I untied one of the parcels for her. Putting her glasses on, she picked up a Bible and tried to read it. She couldn't, and looked at me inquiringly.

' "This is how the Lord has willed it," I said.

' "Praise him," she replied.

'Every year, in a place adjoining her little room, Sister M used to store firewood. That year she had collected more than she needed. I took some of the wood out of the pile and slid the Bibles behind, where the eaves started. Then I put most of the wood back in place, so that no one would suspect anything.

' "Sister M," I told her, "when someone comes from

Romania—a tourist or a visitor, but he must be a man of faith—give him these books. I am sure they will be a great blessing to him. In Romania the thirst for the word of God is as great as it is is here."

'She remained thoughtful for a while and then replied, "I will have to pray that the Lord will send someone to fetch these Bibles."

'I left, not realising that that was to be the last time that I was to see her. It was the Lord's will that we should part, and I left my country, my brothers in Christ, my house—everything, to go into a wider world.' His voice filled with sadness.

'But this is where we need you,' I told him, patting him on the back. But he was still deep in thought. Both of us were silent. I was curious to know what he was thinking. Did he know what had happened to the Bibles after that? Had Sister M written to him?

'Well, brother,' he said, looking into my face again, 'the Lord is wonderful. Let me see, where were we? At the beginning of 1968—in January, I think it was—I received a letter written in the trembling hand of old Sister M. I still treasure it. She wrote, "Brother P, I prayed to the Lord to send me one of his children, and he did! I gave him all the bread, and he was overjoyed. Alleluia!" '

There was a silence as we both gave thanks to God. When I opened my eyes, Brother P put his arm on my shoulder.

'You weren't by any chance the person who took those Bibles from Sister M's attic, were you?'

'No, not I, but the Lord.'

'Alleluia,' we exclaimed, both at the same time—arousing some curiosity in the restaurant.

As we said goodbye at the station the sun was sinking behind the mottled buildings. The town seemed to be already asleep. A cold wind swept the russet leaves along, but in our souls we were filled with boundless praise and gratitude to God.

PART TWO

Yugoslavia

1

I go south

DURING THE years 1967–9 many Romanians were allowed to travel abroad, either to visit relatives and friends,
or simply as tourists.

The desire to go abroad began to grow in me, and I
found my thoughts turning insistently towards Yugoslavia. Ever since childhood I have been attracted by that
country. At school the geography teacher had pointed it
out on the map and had described it with such enthusiasm that I could almost imagine myself basking on the
shores of the Adriatic. I determined that when I grew up
I would save up enough money to go there.

Now my daydreams returned, only to disappear abruptly, just as if someone had torn up a picture postcard
in front of my eyes, and the scene faded to be replaced by
the Word of God. Was God really telling me to go to
Yugoslavia? My thoughts certainly turned in this direction with increasing frequency, and I could not get the
idea out of my mind.

I felt a gentle stirring in my soul, and my enthusiasm
began to increase as I thought back to my Bulgarian
journey. Something told me that the Lord would be with
me on this journey too. I began to feel certain that I
should visit Yugoslavia.

But I was soon brought up against realities. A passport
for Yugoslavia, I remembered, was not at all easy to
obtain. A friend of mine had been trying for several years
to visit his sister in Belgrade, but he had never been
granted permission. I had no compassionate grounds for
an application, no near relatives in that country—no con-

tacts at all. I couldn't even give a guarantee that I would not try to escape. But I still had the Word of God.

The next day I discussed the matter with a colleague at work. He explained, 'It is not impossible to go to Yugoslavia, but once you get there you could always refuse to come back. The authorities are afraid you might do this; so you have to present them with a guarantee that you will return.'

'What guarantee?' I asked. 'Isn't it enough for me to sign a declaration that I will return? I wouldn't think of escaping anyway.'

'I believe you—but they won't. Anyone can make a declaration and then leave. As far as they are concerned, you would have to leave your wife and children here. In general, husbands come back to their wives, and parents come back to their children. But you are a bachelor. What sort of guarantee can you give?'

'You're right. I've no one and nothing to leave behind as a guarantee that I will return. Just my word.'

'And no one will take any notice of that,' he said, somewhat puzzled by my naïveté.

I could see absolutely no possibility of getting a passport. All I wanted was to go for a holiday, travel round a bit and obtain some . . . Bibles. For that no one was prepared to give me a passport.

It seemed that only if no one investigated my application, and if they signed it with their eyes closed, would I stand any chance of getting the necessary papers.

That day I didn't feel at all well. I was disappointed that the dreams which I had cherished for so long should suddenly collapse like a pack of cards. I thought up all sorts of schemes, but none seemed to be workable, and I remained as frustrated as ever. Yet I could not escape the uneasiness in my subconscious, and from time to time the same word kept recurring, definitely and firmly, 'Bibles, Bibles'.

God was speaking to me insistently—and try as I might, I could not escape his call. There was a long struggle going on inside me, and in order to calm myself I reached over and opened my desk drawer, taking out my New Testament.

44

'Lord, what is your will?' I murmured as I opened the book. My eyes fell immediately on the words, 'The angel of the Lord spoke to Philip, saying, Get up and go south.' Closing the book I accepted that it was his will that I should go.

But how, and where exactly? There were still a great many unanswered questions in my mind.

'Lord,' I murmured again, 'show me clearly what your will is. Guide my footsteps, my thoughts, my intentions.' As I got more and more confused and bogged down in uncertainty, a voice thundered in my ear.

'Arise and go!'

I had almost finished my day's work at the office. Still hearing those words, I cleared up and left.

I drove into the centre of town, where I had a small matter of business to see to. The car streaked alongside the tram rails. Then, in spite of my intention to go straight on, something which I cannot explain made me turn the wheel violently to the right, so that I was heading straight towards the police headquarters building.

I parked the car outside and walked in through the heavy, rusty iron gate. There was still half an hour before the place closed. I quickly gathered up the necessary forms and began to fill them in, applying for a passport for a thirty-day stay in Yugoslavia. I went up to the window just before it was due to close and handed in the forms to an official. He read them through carefully.

'What are my chances?' I asked him.

Looking up from the papers, he gazed at me steadily, then turned the page to the section dealing with my family situation, checked with whom I was planning to leave, read out my reasons for going, coughed dryly, rubbed his nose nonchalantly with his index finger and said, 'Pretty slim.' Then, after a pause, he repeated the well-worn formula that is heard by hundreds every day, 'We will let you know our decision.'

I left, somewhat relieved. It was as if a heavy stone had been lifted from my soul. Taking new heart, I greedily drank in the refreshing air of the streets as I drove along. It was the beginning of spring. Under a still pale sun and a grey sky, gypsies were strolling along the streets with bunches of snowdrops and violets, not daring to shout their wares, but from time to time offering their flowers discreetly to passers-by. In a nearby park the brilliant green grass, washed clean in the last fall of snow, was strewn with snowdrops and occasional cherry blossoms.

There followed a long period of waiting, to which I gradually became resigned. Many times I told myself there had been no point in filling in the forms and paying the fee—and yet again and again the words of the Bible came clearly before my eyes and rang in my memory. In my imagination I saw myself setting off for Yugoslavia, sightseeing on the Adriatic and then finding somehow—I didn't know from whom or where—some Romanian Bibles. I could even see the Bibles in the boot of my car as I crossed back over the frontier.

Then I saw myself distributing them, heard the thanks of all those who were going to receive them . . . I was so moved that I fell on my knees in tears and cried out, 'Lord, there are so many brothers, children of yours who do not have your Word. I ask you earnestly to use me and to help me, as only you can.' And once again I experienced that inner calm and certainty, reassured that this was the Lord's work.

Time passed surprisingly swiftly. Weeks went by during which I forgot all about the application. Then one day I came home from work to find a blue envelope on the table and a letter inside with the police stamp on it. 'Your journey to Yugoslavia has been approved.'

I could hardly believe my eyes. I did not know anyone in the police who could have pulled strings in favour of my application. I still have the conviction that it was a direct intervention by God that secured permission for me to go.

At last I was holding in my hand clear proof not only that God approved of my departure, but also that it was he who was sending me. There was now nothing else to do but submit to his will. As I looked back I could see that I had reacted to his leading like a horse not yet broken in. But now his love and understanding had conquered me.

I began to make preparations for my departure ... bought petrol cans, looked the car over and purchased necessities for the journey. I could hardly wait for the holidays. The very thought of visiting a country where anyone is free to go where he likes filled me with excitement. Although, in the back of my mind, there were still many unanswered questions.

Whom was I going to see? Where was I going to sleep? How was I going to fit all the luggage in? What was going to happen when I crossed the border on the way back? These questions became all the more alarming when I considered that I knew no one in Yugoslavia, nor had a single address to go to.

One day, opening my Bible, I read of the astonishing guidance the angel gave to Cornelius to enable him to meet the apostle Peter, and I realised that God was going to guide me in the same way. I knelt down and wept over my hardness of heart.

At the beginning of August, which was a very hot month, the long-awaited holidays arrived. I climbed into the car and set out for Yugoslavia.

I spent that night still in Romania, not far from the frontier, so that I could get an early start the next day. I was very excited, not only at the thought of the impending border check, but also because I realised that in a short time I would be in the country I had dreamed about for so long—and where there were shining new Bibles to be found.

At the frontier there was a long queue of cars stretching in an apparently unending line on both sides of the border. The passport and luggage check proceeded slowly, the overcast sky serving only to emphasise the monotony of the scene.

It was about three hours before my turn came. The officer asked me with a yawn if I was the only person in the car. When I answered in the affirmative, his eyes nearly popped out. He stared at me for a long time, then at the passport, which he handed back, muttering.

Another man opened the boot and looked in my suitcases.

'Where are you going?' he asked suspiciously.

'Yugoslavia.'

'Have you relatives there?' he continued, knowing that as a rule only people who have relatives in that country are allowed to go there.

'Yes, I have. Brothers,' I replied confidently.

'I see.' He glared stonily at me. 'Not many people travel as you are travelling.'

'I'm a delegate,' I said, whispering in his ear as if it were a great secret.

He again looked at me closely, and then said, 'We shall see, sir.' He glanced once more into the car nodded and added nervously, 'you are free to leave. Hurry up or you will cause a jam.'

I heaved a sigh of relief as I drove over to the Yugoslav side. Here the formalities were completed very quickly, and as I went under the barrier I felt as if an enormous burden had been lifted from me.

At that moment I heard someone whisper some words from the Bible in my ear. I turned round abruptly, but there was no one there.

2

An unexpected meeting

THE CAR sped along the winding road bordered with
fields of maize. The engine seemed to be running better
than ever, and I felt a profound and totally inexplicable
joy. Everything around me seemed to join in. Every
breath of wind in the poplar and horse chestnut trees
seemed to be giving me a special welcome.

I pulled up at a spot where the road widened, and
there, at the edge of the road, I thanked the Lord and
asked him once again to lead me and protect me. Then I
set off again, singing at the top of my voice.

The scattered villages rushed past at ever-increasing
speed. But soon the sun began to set lower in the sky, and
the shadows lengthened on the road. Where was I to find
a place to sleep? My pockets were empty except for the
little money I had for petrol.

A host of questions flooded back, but in my happy state
of mind they soon melted away, like snowflakes falling on
a kitchen stove. If the worst came to the worst, I
reasoned, I could always sleep in the car. In the distance I
could see a small town, its lights beginning to shine like
glow-worms.

Noisy crowds thronged the streets in the town centre.
Turning off slightly from the main thoroughfare, I
stopped at the first available parking lot. I don't know
why.

A shop selling car spares caught my eye, and I crossed
the street towards the brightly lit window. Near by was a
hotel, in front of which a group of men were engaged in
noisy discussion. I looked at the things in the window and
was about to move on when I heard a voice call out.

'Look who it is! Come and join us.'

I turned round, but all I could see was a crowd of

people milling around. I looked up the road, but could not locate where the voice had come from. I turned round again, and looked behind me. There was a short man in glasses, waving his right hand and calling to someone. Nobody appeared to be taking any notice.

Then I saw to my surprise that he was coming towards me, motioning me to stop and wait for him. Could it be someone who knew me? I waited for him to catch me up, and when he did so he beamed and embraced me in a bear hug.

I gazed at him mystified, ransacking my memory in an effort to remember where I had seen him before. With much waving and gesticulating, he managed to indicate that he had been to my country and had heard me preach. He had always wanted to meet me, he explained, and now he didn't want to miss the opportunity.

He invited me to the hotel where he was staying, and we sat down at a secluded table. I did not know his language and he did not know mine, but there was much that he wanted to say. In the conversation that ensued I am sure it was only the Lord's intervention that enabled us to understand each other. We used gestures, mime and anything else that came to mind.

Pointing heavenwards, he gave me to understand that as he was travelling along the Lord had directed him to come to this small town and seek out this hotel as a place to put up for the night. He had no idea why he should come here, and had just been asking the Lord for a further revelation of his will.

He went on to say, tapping the table with his finger, that he had reason to believe that I was short of money, and dipping his hand into his wallet he handed me some Yugoslav notes. While he continued to gesticulate and talk rapidly, my soul sent up a prayer of thanks to God.

Those were the first Yugoslav banknotes that I had ever held in my hand. I needed to buy petrol, food and some spare parts for the car—and I had had almost no money.

Silently we both bowed in prayer over the hotel table, each thanking the Lord in his own language. When we raised our heads again we looked at each other for a long time, as if each of us had never thought it possible that we would see the other again. Pushing his glasses up on to his forehead, he began to say something more. I shrugged my shoulders to show that I had not understood; so he drew a notebook from his pocket and with his pencil drew an arrow, above which he wrote a question mark, pointing at the same time towards me. I shrugged my shoulders again. I wanted him to understand that I had no idea where I was going, that I had no precise aim in view.

His eyes opened wide in incredulity. He took off his glasses and looked at me for a long time. Then he patted me on the back, said something in his own language and laughed heartily. He thought for a moment, and then went on, 'Address?'

I looked at him, nonplussed. He repeated the word, then took an address book out of his pocket and indicated that he was asking if I had an address to go to—somewhere I could sleep. By gestures I told him I hadn't.

He began to skim through the book, then tore out a page and wrote down an address. The town was quite near, and the name he had written seemed familiar too. He explained, pointing first at me and then at the address, that I would find a place to sleep there—and be able to obtain some Bibles.

I couldn't believe my ears and eyes. When he wrote a Bible text next to the address I jumped inwardly for joy and pressed his hand into mine with all my strength.

I was gradually beginning to understand God's plan.

Later, when just the two of us were left in the hotel lobby, it became clear that I was not going to be able to reach the address he had given me that night, and he asked me what I would do. I said I would probably sleep in the car. But the Lord was not going to permit even this minor discomfort. It transpired that a friend of my companion's had for some unknown reason failed to turn up, but there was a room reserved in the hotel for him. It was at my disposal.

As I lay on my back on the hotel bed, my eyes still

open, thinking about all that God had done that day, I realised what it means in a practical way to have God as your God, and to commit your whole future into his hands.

3

The house with the green gate

THE FIRST rays of the early morning sun had begun to
penetrate the rain-streaked window. As I opened my eyes
and looked out, I thought the day looked like a blub-
bering child rubbing its eyes.

I got up and knocked on the door of the adjoining
room, but there was no one there. As I sat on the edge of
the hotel bed the events of the previous day seemed like a
dream. But the piece of paper with the address was still
there on the table—the large letters printed in blue
crayon, with the Bible verse twice underlined.

As I stared at it I remembered that I now had some
money, and I began to toy with the idea of making a trip
to the Adriatic, seeing the sights in a few towns and then,
on my way back, visiting the address to which I had been
directed. It seemed an attractive plan.

I looked at the map, calculated the distance involved
and decided then and there to set off. The car coasted
effortlessly along, past fields and woods, up hill and down
dale, through the ever-changing countryside. I was in
high spirits and hummed a tune—'How great thou art'—
as I went along.

Hours went by. The sullen, unceasing rain sent a gentle
warmth into my body. The road stretched monotonously
in front of me, and I felt a weight in all my limbs. My
eyelids became heavier and heavier, and I began to picture in my mind's eye the coast and all the famous
beauty spots. I held the wheel with one hand as I rubbed
my eyes vigorously.

Suddenly I noticed what looked like a brightly
coloured signboard apparently moving along in front of
me. A whole row of letters in different colours spelled out
the words, 'Bibles, Bibles, Bibles . . .'

The vision—or whatever it was—compelled my attention. Light played upon the letters, bringing out the varied colours. The car seemed to be driven by some unseen hand, veering first to the right and then to the left while I gazed spellbound at the changing colours in front of me.

I came to my senses as the vision faded. I felt as if my hair was standing on end, and a cold shudder shook me from head to foot. I rubbed my eyes again and looked ahead, still expecting to see the dancing letters. But there was only the shining wet road surface, stretching endlessly before me.

In the afternoon the haze of clouds that filled the sky began to disperse, like an enormous piece of dirty, torn gauze. I looked, now at the road stretching into the distance, now at the clouds as they drifted into various weird shapes.

I was in high spirits again. Every trace of tiredness had disappeared as the sky cleared to reveal in the distance the sun shining out from between great blobs of grey clouds, against a background of azure blue. At the edge of a wood I stopped to give the engine a rest, and to have a bite to eat. I was not hungry. It was really just for something to do that I rummaged round in my luggage, then ate the food I had left.

I still do not know whether what I had seen was a vision from the Lord, wishful thinking or just a product of my imagination. But as I consider the events that followed, one thing is sure: the Lord was making it plain to me that he had brought me into Yugoslavia primarily to obtain Bibles.

I saw then, as at so many other times in my life, that, almost without realising it, I was obstinate and hardhearted even when God's will had been revealed. When he wanted me to go in one direction, I insisted on going in the other until such time as, tired of my useless resistance, I fell to my knees, bowed my head and said, 'You have won, Lord. I can see what your will is.' As I thanked him my whole being was invigorated. I felt like a bird that had been let out of a cage.

At the first fork in the road I took a left turn, which brought me gradually back in the opposite direction. It was not long before I came to a sign which told me I was quite near the town named on my piece of paper. The shadows began to lengthen on the whitish asphalt, and I looked eagerly at each signpost as I sped by. Then in the distance the outline of the town grew clearer.

It was a clean town, with wide, straight, quiet streets. I drove in slowly, deep in thought, past the pale glow of the street-lighting. In the town centre I asked the way. I soon found myself on a street with wide pavements, lined with laburnum trees whose leaves were just turning yellow. I parked the car underneath one of the biggest of them.

I sat for a little while, looking at the dark green gate which bore the number I knew. A few people passed me on the other side of the street, crossed over and went through the gate. Then two old men, supporting each other as they walked along, passed me on the left and entered. I heard snatches of conversation, and then silence descended again.

Suddenly it dawned on me that the Lord had wanted me to come to the house that day. I went towards the 'house of prayer' with the same eager expectation as always, and waited. Soon two ladies came along, and I slipped discreetly in behind them.

At the other end of the entrance hall there was a flight of stairs leading up to a large open door. A man stood there with a big smile on his face. He was holding a Bible and he stretched his hand out to me with the same greeting that he gave to everyone. I made a gesture to the effect that I didn't understand his language, that I was a foreigner.

For a moment neither of us said a word. Then I took out the scrap of paper with the address on it and showed it to him. He studied the writing, trying to make out the signature under the Bible reference, then motioned me into a corner of the courtyard outside. And there, for some reason, we could understand each other, though we were each speaking in our own language. An unseen interpreter was obviously helping us.

It was not long before I found myself in a spacious room, full of people. At the front was a pulpit, and behind me a text in large letters.

After prayers and hymns, some of which I recognised, the man next to me stood up, went to the pulpit—and introduced me to the congregation. I stood up, blushing bright red.

With faltering steps and anxious heart I made my way forward. I had no idea what I was expected to do. How could I speak to them if I didn't know their language?

As I entered the pulpit, the congregation rose. The brother motioned to me to read a text, and I obeyed mechanically. He saw the uncertainty in my eyes, and managed to convey that he expected me to preach a sermon. I stood for a moment as if turned to stone—then made hesitant signs to the effect that I needed a translator.

'*Bog i ja*,' he replied—God and I will.

I opened the New Testament, and turned the pages. In Luke's gospel my eyes lighted on the story of the rich young ruler. I showed the brother the verses to read. As he read the passage through, slowly and gently, I seemed to see before me in white letters on purple: 'What must I do to inherit eternal life?'

Then another hymn. Soon I would have to preach—what was I going to say? I bowed my head and lifted my soul to God, murmuring, 'Lord, you see me in front of all these people who cannot understand my language and whom I hardly know. Please use me as your interpreter, so that these men may understand your Word, and your will for them.'

As the echo of this prayer sounded through my soul I could see before me an enormous bright silver screen, and on it appeared ideas on which I could build the content of my sermon. I read it all, and it remained wonderfully clear. 'The basic problem in the life of every man is to obtain eternal life.' The line seemed to be wiped off the screen as soon as I had read it. 'The only person who can solve the problem of eternal life is Jesus Christ.'

As one line appeared, the previous one vanished. But

they all built up to a logical whole—sentences, ideas and propositions of an unforgettable clarity. I was so absorbed reading them that I didn't realise the singing had stopped.

I started as the brother next to me gently nudged me. Then I stood up, feeling as if my whole face was aglow with radiance.

At first my translator spoke slowly, searching for the right words, but as I got under way he spoke more and more fluently, until he was speaking about as fast as I was, completely confident. After a time I realised that I, too, was no longer searching for words and expressions. I was able to speak to the congregation as to a friend. And yet, in a way, I did not seem to be the one who was speaking.

As I came to the end of my sermon I felt more and more empty, as if the last of the water was being poured out of the jug. My voice became steadier and calmer, the tone more subdued, my gestures more restrained.

I remained standing for a few moments, then fell on my knees, exhausted, behind the pulpit. Everyone else in the room knelt with me, and there was a stir like the murmur in a beehive. It was as if everyone there was pouring out his soul to God in tears and repentance, as to one who was very near, waiting to receive them and bless them.

During that long time of prayer I felt myself gradually returning to normal, to the same man I had always been—timid, fearful lest I should say the wrong thing. I felt at the same time relieved, yet empty, a mixture of happiness and fearfulness and delightful insignificance.

The next day I was invited to look round my friend's office. Absorbed by a duplicating machine, I didn't notice him slip behind a faded canvas curtain. The crash of falling books made me spin round; there at my feet lay a heap of brand-new Bibles, glistening like pearls in the autumn sun.

Behind the curtain there were more Bibles than I had seen in my life. All I could see were the edges, protruding from torn packets—a beautiful sight. The fat cheeks of my host creased in a broad smile of happiness.

I picked up one of the Bibles, my hand trembling with emotion. It was printed in Romanian. My eyes shifted from its pages to the packets and back again: I was bubbling with excitement. As if I were watching a film sequence, I could see passing before my eyes little churches in the mountainous regions of Bucovina and Transylvania—churches of all shapes and sizes crowded with believers, all with their hands stretched out for Bibles.

Then, as abruptly as if someone had pressed a switch, I was back in the old attic in Bulgaria, and I heard the thunder of the same voice I had heard then: 'I will never leave you nor forsake you.'

I jumped. My host looked at me oddly, and his insistent stare made me feel uncomfortable. He was no doubt wondering whether I was the person to whom he could entrust his treasure—the Bibles.

'They are all for you,' he whispered slowly. 'Will you take them?'

I remained silent, sunk in thought. How many would go in the boot of the car, and how many in the car itself? I could put a lot in the boot. I could see myself packing them in and making light-heartedly for the frontier.

But the frontier crossing bothered me. Already I could visualise the car—Bibles everywhere. My joy, which increased in proportion to the number of Bibles that could be crammed in, was dampened as I envisaged the luggage search, the inquisitive looks and endless questions.

'I'll take as many as I can manage,' I said, explaining through gestures what I had in mind. We knelt down on the floor, and I sought the Lord's guidance in deciding what I should take, and how I should arrange the luggage. I asked for especial protection at the border crossing.

I rose from my knees with a new peace and vitality.

The next few days I spent resting, walking, and travelling from town to town, from mountains to coast and back again. But the date for my return to Romania was fast approaching, and each day I prayed for protection at the border. When I did this, I remembered my return from Bulgaria, and how the Lord had kept me then.

My spirit would again become calm, and I would sing with all my heart, conscious of a direct contact with God.

4

A precious load

LEAVING behind the coast with its warm sand and shady trees I returned to the laburnums and the green gate. My friends had been expecting me the day before, and were rather anxious. That night we prayed together, asking God to confirm his will and—again—to grant protection at the frontier.

I spent a sleepless night—still worried, still looking for a sign. I watched the sky grow light, and the first rays of sun reflect from the windscreens of passing cars on to the ceiling of my room. I was convinced that the Lord had not answered my prayers—and at the same time knew that I lacked faith.

My eyes refused to close, and my thoughts kept returning to my imminent departure. What was I going to do? What was I going to say? As in a flashback I saw all that had happened on my return from Bulgaria, and my courage returned. God had protected me then as I carried his Word, and he would protect me again. Little by little, I calmed down, and at last I fell asleep.

Next day, as I made my preparations, I was still tense and uncertain. My host kept a wary eye on me. Obviously he wanted me to take as many Bibles as possible, but he also feared for me. Soon all my personal luggage had been loaded—but we stood there in an uneasy silence. What about the Bibles?

'Let's pray, brother,' I suggested. We went indoors and knelt in front of the stack of Bibles. When we rose from our knees, I was sure.

'I'll take the lot,' I said firmly.

He looked at me, nodding slowly in agreement. I filled the boot with Bibles, and put more behind the back seat and in the passenger's seat. A tarpaulin covered them all.

The long shadows of evening were already creeping across the cobbles of the courtyard as we finished. I searched in my pockets for the key to lock the door, and pulled out a Yugoslav banknote. I showed it to my friend. The shops would soon be closing; so I had to hurry.

In the first shop window I saw an electrical appliance. I don't know why it attracted me, but I thought it would be useful at home, and so I went inside, tried it out and bought it. I threw it on to the back seat, next to the Bibles, and the packing tore open to reveal gleaming metal.

Before we went indoors, I turned and embraced my host, thanking him in the name of all the Christians in my country for his wonderful gift. Under the light of a street lamp our eyes shone with inexpressible joy—the joy of a sower who anticipates the reaping. Then we joined together to give praise and thanks to God, and I do not doubt that from that moment on celestial beings surrounded the car and accompanied me for the rest of my journey.

There was complete silence during supper. I forgot about going to bed, letting my gaze drift instead into space ... and I found myself face to face with border guards and customs officials. On this occasion they were particularly strict, rummaging mercilessly through the suitcases of travellers. Trembling in every limb, I drove up and opened the doors. They asked me to open the boot. One of them lifted up the tarpaulin, gave a cry of surprise, and a terrible pressure bore down on my throat.

'Lord, Lord,' I cried, 'it's your Word. They can't do that. Please intervene.' Perhaps I didn't shout aloud because my host apparently did not hear me.

Still trembling and unsure whether I was still experiencing a vision or had returned to reality, I seemed to see a curtain drawn back, and in front of me a huge crowd, dressed in the various regional styles of my country. They were all coming towards me with hands outstretched, with intent expressions on their faces and eyes aglow, shouting for Bibles.

I tried to run and hide. I swerved off to the right and to

the left, but each time they blocked my path. I could not shake them off. Then I looked down—and saw a large open suitcase, crammed full of Bibles.

A pleasant warmth suffused my body. I began to take Bibles out of the suitcase and hand them out left and right. And as fast as I did so, the case filled up again. More and more people crowded round, and at last I fell on the suitcase, exhausted.

5

A battle with fear

THE SUN shone high: there was not a cloud to be seen. It could not be far to the border. I thought of my host's promise to pray for me and of my regretful farewell that morning to the family who had been so good to me.

I slowed down, realising that these were my last hours in Yugoslavia. All my natural fear came surging back, and a cold shudder went through me. My hands trembled on the wheel, forcing me to reduce speed still more.

Alongside a field of maize I pulled up and opened the bonnet to cool the engine. Leaving the car, I walked into the field for about fifty paces and fell on my knees. Around me were thousands of heads of corn, rocking to and fro like duelling swordsmen whenever the wind stirred. There seemed to be agitation all around—a tremor going through the whole field.

I raised my hands to heaven and, in a voice choked with emotion, cried to the Lord. My words mingling with the rustle of the corn swaying in the winds, I prayed as one who feels he is about to be swallowed up by the earth. I was desperately seeking help—urgent help. My voice was crackled, my tongue rolled round in my mouth, my throat was as dry as tinder, and my words came out with increasing difficulty.

There in that lonely maize field near the border I learned what it means to be consumed by prayer, to pray on until one is assured of victory. It was then that I discovered that in my deepest being there were inexhaustible springs, unsuspected power which must be squeezed out to spill forth in the presence of heaven, the angels and God.

My eyes streamed with tears, and my overflowing soul had to be poured out—and the more I poured it out before God, the deeper I had to go. I was oblivious of time and of my surroundings: I was alone in God's presence. I knew he was looking at me; I could feel the fire of his piercing gaze, and my prayer became more and more fervent.

It was as if my voice passed out of my control, and I knew that I had begun to pray directly with my spirit. I don't know whether I prayed in my own language or in another, but I know that my mind became more and more surprised at what was coming out of my mouth. I had no doubt that I was in direct contact with heaven, with its glory and the heavenly hosts, and with Jesus the Saviour.

I felt no longer limited to time, but outside it, in the antechamber of heaven.

I was exhausted—yet overwhelmed with a deep and gentle peace. The sun had climbed high, and its rays beat down on my forehead. The maize was still swaying in the breeze. My eyes and cheeks were wet with tears, and my shirt soaking. Exhausted, I repeated the words which had always been my shield: 'Lord, protect your Word. I am powerless, and I don't know how. I have done all I can. The rest is up to you.'

When I rose from my knees I saw two deep impressions in the soil, and found that my trousers were covered with red ants ... but not one had bitten me. Behind me a swarm of ants from the same anthill had been using my sandals as a springboard for their manoeuvres, and I watched them as they milled around the hot metal of the buckle.

I looked at the car, then towards the frontier, then back at the ants. Everything spoke in its own particular language of the goodness of God.

As I left the maize field behind I felt strangely refreshed. It was as if I had come out of a cold shower—an inner shower, pleasant to the soul and spirit, in which every fibre of my nervous system had been washed clean. All was calm, peaceful and transparent.

Quiet had descended on my soul. As I saw the yellow border buildings come into sight, not even a gun fired behind me would have made me jump. If only I had succeeded in retaining such composure later, what exhaustion, trouble, frayed nerves and anxiety I could have saved myself.

As I approached the frontier the traffic speeded up, and the number of cars increased. I was the only one coasting lazily along, singing as I went. Passengers turned to look at me as they went past, and from a Romanian car an unfamiliar voice shouted, 'Hurry up there!' His words faded in the roar of another vehicle coming up behind.

The heat was stifling. In front of me was a Renault, heavily laden and dusty, with four people crammed inside. The driver opened the door, got out and stood there for a moment, then came across to me. It was the man who had passed me earlier and told me to hurry up. Friendly as all Romanians are in foreign countries, he wasted no time on formalities, but launched straight into conversation.

'So it's back to the grindstone again! Where are you from?'

I wasn't particularly anxious to talk. I would have liked to have been left alone to concentrate on my own thoughts and to pray quietly, so that I could arm myself against the ordeal of the border crossing.

The man standing in front of me had a round, bronzed face, brown as an autumn leaf. His eyes were hidden behind black, bushy eyebrows.

'All good things come to an end,' he remarked coming nearer. Craning his neck, he peered into the car. 'I see that you have a lot of luggage.'

'As much as any tourist.'

'You know,' he commented looking at my recent purchase on the back seat, 'I saw a machine just like that, in a shop window. My wife would have liked one, but I hadn't enough money left.'

'Oh, well . . .'

'I see your car is full of packets. What have you got in them?'

'I have in them,' I said, 'what any tourist would have

bought for his friends and acquaintances—of which I have many.'

'That must have cost a bit,' he said, dashing for his car as the line moved up. I started the engine and edged forward. Everything seemed to be happening excruciatingly slowly. I switched off the engine again to save petrol. The man with the Renault came over for another chat.

'How was it last time?' he asked, nodding in the direction of the frontier.

'All right.'

'What do you mean, all right?' he insisted, rather annoyed that I hadn't taken his question too seriously.

'It was all right,' I repeated. 'You'll see. We'll go slowly forward until we come to the border guards. First we will stop on the Yugoslav side, and they will want to look at our passports. Their customs will not assume we are anything but straightforward tourists, and let us through. Then we come to the barrier, and on to Romanian territory. Our fellow-Romanians will come up, and we will show them our passports, and they will ask us some questions. And of course we will tell them we haven't anything of importance, and they will be reassured. Then comes the more difficult part—the Romanian customs.

'Because you have a larger and heavier car they will put me on the left and you on the right. Then two customs officers will come out—one for you and one for me. They will ask for our customs declarations, which they will look at, and then will come the fatal question: "Have you anything to declare?"

'As you reply they will see that you are apprehensive, and they will ask you to get out of the car, to lift the seats up. They will look underneath the back seat and in the boot, but they will leave me in peace. Then they will pat me on the back and say, "Good boy; you can go, as you have nothing in your car."'

When he heard this, the man leaned over again, looked at the packets and interrupted. 'You're having me on,' he said, and returned to his car.

At the barrier I was overcome with another fit of trembling. My cheeks flushed bright red, and the courage that

I had felt in my conversation with the man in the Renault a short while ago began to fade.

The Yugoslav border guards and customs would probably not even want to look in the car, I told myself. But what if one of them, out of sheer curiosity, should glance through the windscreen? What would he say if he saw all those packets? Surely he would motion the car aside and ask me to open them. I remembered that not long ago a tourist had been turned back at the border because he had some Bibles.

What would they do with me? Would they confiscate my car and make me return empty handed? I thought that was unlikely, because I hadn't really attempted to conceal anything. Everything was quite open. In such a case, I knew, they would only confiscate the goods seized. And then, what? Probably they would turn me and the car, with all the Bibles displayed, over to the Romanian authorities.

The thought appalled me. It seemed impossible that I would not escape prosecution. In a state of great nervous tension I rested my head on the steering wheel and, hummed a tune in order to calm myself.

The driver of the Renault turned round to look at me from time to time, probably to see how my courage was faring. He was discussing something with his wife.

As I hummed, the vision of the night before came back to me. And a gentle breath of wind—calm, soothing and mysterious—filled the whole of my being.

6

Surrounded by angels

THE SUN was sinking to the right of the column of ve-
hicles as I followed the red car in front of me through the
barrier. My heart beat faster. Crossing the Romanian
border is an unnerving experience, even if you have
nothing to hide: the mere fact of having to submit to a
search is unpleasant.

I saw the man with the Renault snatch his passport
from the Yugoslav customs official and go round to open
the boot of his car, but the official motioned to him not to
bother. The driver turned and nodded at me with a smile
which soon disappeared when he looked towards the
Romanian side of the border. I had gone tense again, but
I pulled myself together and managed a smile when the
customs man came up to me and addressed me in broken
Romanian.

'Your holiday is over?'

'Yes, unfortunately. What a beautiful country you
have.'

'I don't suppose you have anything forbidden in your
car?'

'Oh no,' I said emphatically, feigning surprise. 'Absolutely nothing to declare.'

Apparently satisfied, he smiled and quickly stamped
my customs declaration. Without delay I crossed over to
the Romanian checkpoint and found myself face to face
with the customs and border guards of my own country. I
was as taut as a cord about to snap.

The guards checked my passport, while one of the
customs men came forward and motioned me to pull the
car over. At that moment I caught sight of the man in the
Renault, watching a tall officer rummage through his luggage. The man, his wife and children were standing about

uneasily, unhappy about the search that was being conducted. The driver was nervously trying to explain something to the official.

I switched off the engine. The customs man came towards me carrying a brown briefcase underneath his arm. I felt as if the whole earth was fleeing in front of me. He stopped and turned as a colleague called to him. I got out and quickly unlocked the boot, then stood nonchalantly in front of the open door of the car, waiting for him to make the first move. In order to look as natural as possible, I began to wipe the windscreen with a cloth, all the while praying silently, 'Now, more than at any other time, my fate depends on you. Please protect your Word—I can do nothing more.'

'Your declaration, please,' said the official, with a salute and smile. He could see that I was nervous. 'Why get so flustered when you haven't got any weapons or drugs? I can see that you have nothing to do with either.'

I turned bright scarlet, but the officer went on good-naturedly checking the declaration.

'Gold: no? Jewels: no? Foreign currency: no?'

'That's right. I never even had any pocket money!'

'We are not to blame for that,' he said, looking at me more closely.

'I didn't say you were . . .' I began, only to be cut short.

'So what have you to declare?'

'See for yourself. Just small things. The whole car is open for your inspection. Go ahead.'

'Mmm,' he murmured, frowning as if in an effort to remember something. Perhaps he was trying to recall whether my name figured on one of his lists of suspicious people. Perhaps an order had been given to search the car thoroughly.

Suddenly his face brightened. He bent over slightly, bringing his face close to mine, and peered into the boot. A pair of red-hot tongs seized my heart, and my mind seemed to be clouded in a thick fog. For a moment I could see nothing—nothing at all. Then I saw the face of my Yugoslav friend, praying for me as I crossed the frontier. 'Lord . . .' I managed to squeeze out silently, but I was interrupted.

'I can see that you have nothing in the boot. I don't suppose you have anything in the spare wheel, either?' The officer, stared at me hard.

'Hardly.'

'You know,' he said, 'we have had cases of people filling their spare wheel with . . . Bibles. But that didn't wash. We've had years of experience, and we know all the tricks.'

'I can well believe that.'

He folded up the declaration, which he had stamped, put it in his briefcase and then looked inside the car.

'You know, I like that machine, I really do,' he remarked, indicating the appliance I had bought.

I hardly heard him; I was already lost in thought. I was thinking of wheels stuffed with Bibles, of the fact that he had so much experience, that nothing had escaped his attention and nothing would. His words echoed in my ears, 'I can see you have nothing in the boot.'

The boot was crammed full of books, exactly as I had packed them just before setting out. I was so flabbergasted I almost forgot that he was standing right next to me.

'What are you thinking about? The children? It won't be long before you see them again. Make sure you get home soon.'

He looked inside the car again at the gadget that had taken his fancy—this time through the back door. I was transfixed. This, I felt, was the end. I pictured in my imagination those thousands of hands stretching out to me.

The customs officer reached into the car and twisted one of the switches on the machine. But the door got in his way, and he shut it noisily.

'Yes, that machine must have cost you something,' he said. 'Worth going to Yugoslavia just to get it.'

'Yes,' I replied, thinking he intended to confiscate it.

'If you had anything else, of course, I would charge

70

you duty . . .' He turned his attention back again to the boot.

I do not know if the angels of God came and whisked away the car for a few seconds, or whether a mist blinded the customs official. I don't know now, and I didn't know then. I wasn't concerned at the time to work out how the miracle happened; it was enough to know that the Lord had performed it.

I am quite certain that as the customs man approached the car there was a host of angels around us. I believe that if anyone had touched those Bibles he would have dropped dead on the spot. They were like the mountain in the Old Testament, surrounded by a wall of fire which no one could approach unless he was sanctified.

The customs officer, apparently bored by now, turned his attention to a Ford that was pulling up behind me.

'Have a good journey.' He nodded his dismissal, adding, 'You have a splendid machine.'

I stood there as if turned to stone, with my back to the car, gazing vacantly into the distance. I was not entirely aware of my surroundings. I had such a strange sensation—a mixture of relief, astonishment and gratitude. A feeling of lightness spread through me, bringing an indescribable happiness and peace to my whole being.

'Hey, you! Get going!' I came round to hear a shout from the customs man, who was gesticulating from the other side of the Ford. I slammed the boot shut, took the steering wheel and pulled out slowly, my foot trembling on the accelerator.

I parked the car at the edge of the road and opened the doors to rest for a while and recover my strength. Gradually I unwound, as a bowstring goes slack after use. A blanket of drowsiness and limpness spread over on me, urging me to sleep. My eyelids grew heavy, and my eyes began to smart. The sun, now low down in the sky, seemed to shoot its rays at me like thousands of golden needles.

I washed my eyes at a spring to try and keep awake. My arms were so tired that I could hardly move them, and as I peered at my face in the car mirror I could see that it was as pale as wax. I looked as if I had just been discharged after a long stay in hospital. I seemed to have aged terribly.

But slowly I recovered, regaining my self-control, and peace flooded my soul. It was as if a storm had ceased. I started the car again, singing as I went along, wishing that my Yugoslav brother could have heard my song of praise and victory. To experience God's miraculous dealings at first hand was a profoundly moving experience.

Not much further on I passed the Renault, parked on the dusty grass verge. The driver signalled to me to stop, and I pulled in just past him. His wife, too, came towards me.

'Tell me,' said the man, 'are you a prophet or a fortune teller?'

'Neither,' I replied, rather taken aback.

'Then how is it that everything went exactly as you told me it would?'

'I don't know,' I said, 'but I do know that I am one of the smallest and least significant of God's children.'

His eyes widened in amazement, and he stared first at me and then at his wife, who had come a little closer in order to get a good look at this 'miracle worker'.

'What's that?' asked the man.

'It means,' I said, 'to entrust oneself completely, in whatever situation, into the hands of God. You know, Jesus Christ died for our sins. Through his sacrifice we can find forgiveness, salvation and redemption. If we accept him, he loves us and protects us. When we die, he brings us into his eternal and glorious kingdom.'

The two gazed at me in greater and greater amazement. He kept looking at my radiant face, followed closely every one of my gestures, and listened to every word with rapt attention. I paused.

'Wouldn't you like to become his children too? All you have to do is accept Jesus as your personal Lord and Saviour.'

The man and his wife looked at each other. Both seemed at a loss.

'We believe in God too,' the man began, wrinkling his sweat-covered forehead. 'But there are many times when a person has to go against his conscience. I'm a Communist party member . . . I have to say that I don't believe.'

'That makes no difference, comrade,' I said. 'Jesus Christ died on the cross for Communists as well. He will accept party members.'

'Yes, yes,' he said, nodding. Then the couple went back to their car. He waved me a curt goodbye, and a few moments later his car flashed by me.

I cruised cheerfully along the winding road. I was on the lookout for a place to stop again, as I was burning with impatience to thank the Lord. I passed a row of horse chestnut trees and old acacias, their strangely sawn-off shapes silhouetted against the evening sky. Here and there I could see patches of yellow leaves: it was already autumn. The air became calmer and cool.

I pulled over on to a grassy space between two trees, then crossed the road into a field. In a slight clearing between the rows of maize, I knelt and raised my voice to God. It was a prayer of victory and thanksgiving, from a heart deeply touched by the mercy and loving-kindness of God.

I am totally convinced that God delights especially to answer prayer made to him in impossible situations. He is pleased when we go out on a limb with him—when we commit our whole destiny into his hands, so that we depend entirely upon his love. It is then that he can show his mighty power and stretch forth his hand to deliver us.

And when we see how God protects and saves us, we no longer need anyone to tell us what he is like. We do not need to see his face, because we know his mighty acts of power, and in these he is revealed.

7

The rocket

IT SEEMED as though the night would never end. The railway compartment was too warm, and the corridor too cold; so I kept flitting restlessly from one to the other. I peered out of the window into the darkness. In the compartment everyone else was sound asleep.

I felt uneasy: I was travelling to a town where I didn't know a single address. I had passed through it only once before. The man I had to meet worked in an office somewhere near the railway station, but the train was due to arrive at 4.30 in the morning. Where could I go at such an unearthly hour?

On the horizon a thin white line announced the arrival of dawn. I knew it was the Lord who had brought me here, and God had his reasons, yet I still hesitated to embark on this fresh venture. But it was too late to go back now.

A ray of light entered the compartment; day was breaking on the horizon. The white line grew broader and broader, and I watched spellbound.

As the train pulled into the station I could see that the platforms were almost deserted. The few passengers who did get out rapidly disappeared. The train gave a hoarse whistle and moved off.

I could hardly drag the suitcase along. After only a few steps I was obliged to stop for a rest and to change hands; a few steps further, and I had to stop again. At last I reached the grimy waiting room. In the corner was a narrow bench, on which was stretched out a tall man in a filthy shirt. He was snoring like a horse.

Dragging the suitcase, I made for the other corner, and settled down to wait. I was suddenly very aware of the nearness of God, and felt him looking down at me. I burst into tears, then pulled myself together and went on praying.

The man on the other bench seemed gradually to become aware that there was somebody else in the room. He turned over a few times, then sat up and looked at me through half opened eyes.

'What's the matter?' he asked in a kindly voice.

I didn't reply—and now I couldn't restrain my tears. It was as if all the impurities in my soul were being expelled.

'Have you missed the train?'

'No,' I replied. 'I haven't missed the train. Just lost the time.'

'The time? Can I help you at all?'

Rubbing my eyes, I looked up and saw that he was a man of dark complexion, quite old and with a long beard.

'Leave me alone,' I grunted irritably, and looked away. But immediately I regretted my words. 'Forgive me; forgive me, old fellow. I'm so depressed. Only God can understand me. Thank you for . . .'

'I just wanted to help you. There will be another train in two hours' time,' he said.

'Thank you, thank you. Can you tell me where the left-luggage office is?'

'It's on the other side.' Then he saw that I was having trouble with my suitcase. 'Let me give you a hand,' he offered. 'Have you come from Bucharest?'

We both grabbed hold of the handle.

'Let me take it, mate. I'm stronger than you are,' he insisted, taking the case and hurrying on ahead of me. I was grateful that the Lord had sent me a helper; I was exhausted from lack of sleep.

The man in charge of the left-luggage office had dozed off. There were only two other cases in the whole office. When I woke him up, he stared stupidly at me and yawned.

I took my suitcase from the old man. 'Thank you. You have been a great help to me.' I took out a ten-lei note and held it out to him. The man took it nervously, yet eagerly.

'Thanks a lot, mate. I was wondering what I was going to do. I was down to my last sou. There was no bread at home. I haven't eaten for two days.'

'Wait a minute, I have something to tell you,' I said as he turned to leave.

'What else do you want me to do?'

'Believe in Jesus Christ.'

He stopped in his tracks. Taking advantage of his surprise I spoke to him about the forgiveness of sin and eternal life, and he looked at me, troubled.

'What about us gypsies? Can we get to heaven?'

'Yes, because Jesus died for you too. He wants to forgive you and accept you, just as he does everyone else.'

'But no one wants anything to do with us.'

'Jesus needs you as well as me.'

He thought for a while, then asked, 'Have you got a Bible?' A pause. 'I've never seen one.'

'Do you know how to read?' I asked, fingering the new Bible in my pocket.

'A little, but only slowly. My son is in the third class at school, though, and he is learning to read well—he's the best pupil of all the gypsies in the school.'

Cautiously, I handed him a Bible, tucking it underneath a tear in his coat. He understood. Without asking me any more questions, he moved away, saying, 'Thank you. I must go to church as well . . . and I'll pray.'

When the town began to stir into life, I left the station and headed for the town centre in the freshness of the autumn morning, asking directions from the first man I saw who did not seem to be in a hurry.

'Ask for the hospital,' he said. 'The office you're looking for must be somewhere round there.'

Near the hospital I found it. The porter looked at me closely and pointed to a yellow building set back among the trees. I knocked on the door, only to be told that the man I wanted was out. I could wait for him, but no one knew how long he would be.

'We hope he'll be back at two. Why don't you take a walk round our town?'

So I went back along the street lined with horse chest-nut trees, praying that the Lord would see me through. As I walked deep in thought, I asked him to give me another sign that the place where I was and the person I planned to see were according to his will—and that he would guide my steps. Totally absorbed by my anxiety, my gaze fixed on the ground, I turned a corner and collided with a man coming in the opposite direction.

'I do beg your pardon,' I blurted out, looking up. But then I stood there speechless, hardly able to believe my eyes. It was the very man I had been seeking.

Recovering from our astonishment, we stood staring at each other.

'Yes, it's me,' I said with a smile. 'Can you believe it?'

'So,' he sighed, 'at last you have put in an appearance in these parts, brother. I hope you are not in too much of a hurry, and can stay with us for a few days?'

'I wish I were not in a hurry,' I replied. 'I was just wondering how I could reach you as quickly as possible, have time to chat with you and get to the evening service. After that I'm afraid I shall have to leave.'

'But we see you so seldom. You always seem to be in a hurry.' He seemed worried, and I asked him what was troubling him.

'Oh, nothing serious,' he said, almost apologetically. He talked slowly and rarely finished his sentences. Now he hesitated, as if trying to remember something.

'Well, I'll tell you what I was thinking,' he continued. 'Until now I haven't been able to tell anyone about it. Last night I went to bed early. I fell asleep almost immediately. I never remember ... Even now, I don't know whether I saw a vision or had a dream. Perhaps it was a vision ... very strange ... and the strangest thing was that I have no idea what it meant. An interesting vision, most interesting ...'

He turned to me. 'Brother, I believe that if the Lord gives visions, he must also give interpretations. Isn't that so?'

'Yes, I believe that.'

77

'Perhaps that's why the Lord has sent you,' he exclaimed suddenly—then hesitated again. 'Anyway, I'll tell you what happened.'

'Go on.'

'It was a beautiful night, with a hazy moon. I got out of bed, opened the window ... In the distance I could see the woods, a dark mass. Near by I could hear the rippling of the stream as it flowed down the valley. A breath of wind ... The moon hung yellow and bright like ... A fairy tale atmosphere.

'The stars seemed to shine more and more powerfully. The whole sky seemed brighter than I had ever seen it ... It was just like a fairy tale. I tell you, there was a brightness and beauty about it all that could not be described in words.'

He paused. 'And as I gazed at the scene, drinking in the magic of it, I felt my soul lifted up and exclaimed, "O Lord, the heavens declare your glory!" Suddenly, in the distance, there rose in the sky something like a shining silver ball. It soared with the speed of lightning, came closer and closer and grew bigger and bigger. Then I saw it as a cylindrical shape—a projectile—and it seemed to be heading for my window. I backed away into the centre of the room, still watching.'

He seemed in another world as he told the story, as if he were seeing the vision all over again.

'The thing was moving at a fantastic speed. As it drew near it slowed down, and I could see that there was something written along the side of it. It came lower, and I could see the actual writing, but it was in a foreign language, in characters that I had never seen before. I thought it must have come from a foreign country.

'Then I realised that it was a rocket, just like those I had seen photographs of in magazines. I could see that something was being lowered to me—something which looked like a large suitcase of shining gold. And as I stared at the case, the rocket disappeared. For a few moments I could hear the roar of its engines. The case hit the ground and opened. Inside were books—a lot of them.

'I opened my eyes. I was still in bed. I jumped up, went

over to the window and looked out. The sky was clear and bright. The moon was shining, and the stars . . .'

He stopped for a moment. 'What do you think it means? I have no connection with anyone abroad—I don't know any foreign language. What could the Lord have wanted to tell me in all this?'

Astonished at the way God works, I was smiling broadly. A flood of thanksgiving was going up from my soul. Now I had complete confirmation from heaven that the way I had come was according to the will of God.

My friend was still wrapped up in his vision, lost in thought. Then, as if he had suddenly remembered something, he turned quickly to me.

'You wouldn't have any luggage, brother, by any chance?'

'Yes. At the station.'

'Good. It's better if no one sees us carrying luggage.'

My inner tension had nearly disappeared, but not quite. The suitcase would have to be brought from the station as discreetly as possible, and the Bibles would have to be distributed very carefully. It would be decided that evening.

By this time my friend had come down to earth again. He reached into his pocket and pulled out a piece of crumpled paper to write down an address for me.

'I think it would be good to go to this brother's place,' he said. 'You will find the family very hospitable. You'll be able to rest while I go and make all the arrangements.'

We walked along, each taken up with his own thoughts, until, round the corner in front of us, a man and his wife appeared. They were carrying a large, covered basket and having a lively discussion. As they passed us the man raised his eyes and looked at us in surprise. I could see that my friend was disturbed by this.

'What's the matter?' I asked, when the couple were well past us.

'That man shouldn't have seen us,' he said, and murmured, 'Lord, we are in your hands.'

'Don't worry,' I reassured him. 'The Lord will see us through.'

'I believe that. But we are going to have to change our meeting place. Give me the piece of paper.' Crossing out the address he had written, he turned the paper over and wrote a new address on the other side.

'Look,' he said; 'go to this man and tell him I sent you. You can wait for me there. I'll come when it starts to get dark, and then we'll go to the station to collect your luggage, and see how the Lord leads us.' He spoke quickly and nervously.

'You see, in this small town everybody can spot a stranger. If they see you going in one direction, they won't need anyone to tell them where you're going. If they see you with someone today, the whole town will know about it tomorrow. I'm sorry, but I shall have to leave you to find your own way to the house. It's better that no one sees us walking together.'

By this time he was talking so quickly that I could hardly catch what he was saying. Then he gave me directions and, just as a group of men appeared at the other end of the street, shook my hand discreetly, and we parted.

A flight of cranes flew over the yellowing acacia trees, calling out mournfully to each other. From time to time a sprig of leaves fell on to the pavement.

The address was not hard to find. In front of me a high fence of boards, blackened with age, guarded a narrow courtyard. As I opened the gate, a woman who was tending some flowers looked up, brushing aside a wisp of hair. I gave her a Christian greeting, and she came towards me with arms outstretched.

'I have just been with Brother V,' I said, and she immediately asked me to come in. Two boys, one fair, the other dark, were doing their homework. They came over to shake my hand and bid me welcome.

'Children, the Lord has sent us a guest,' said the woman. 'Let us praise the Lord.' Then she disappeared through a door to the right. The children looked at me as if they were used to guests, and I started to talk to them about their schoolwork. They showed me their exercise books and boasted about their good marks. After a few moments their mother reappeared, carrying a large loaf of bread and a plate with cheese and ham on it.

'You must excuse us, brother,' she said, flushing slightly. 'Just now we have only bread and pig fat. It's a regional speciality. While you're eating I'll go and make up a bed. You'll be able to rest for a while.'

There were no dreams this time, just an endless stretch of black water flowing in front of me. When I awoke, my mind was a blank. The blinds had been drawn, plunging the room into semi-darkness. I felt like turning over and going back to sleep again, but at that moment the door handle turned, and I could make out the tall form of a man in the doorway. I beckoned him in. It was Brother G, the master of the house—and he recognised me.

He had been wanting, he said, to have a chat with me for a long time. Little had he expected to be able to do so in his own home.

Night mingled with day as I left the house with Brother V and made for the station. We walked briskly. We had a lot to do in the next few hours.

I retrieved the suitcase, and Brother V, who had been waiting on the street corner, helped me carry it. But even with the two of us, it was very heavy. Finally, my friend could contain his curiosity no longer.

'What have you got in this suitcase,' he burst out, 'to make it so heavy?'

'Let's say they're rockets,' I replied with a smile, and he fell silent.

Brother V heaved the suitcase over the remaining few yards to the end of the courtyard where he lived. We went in through the open door, hands ready to drop off from taking the weight. We carried the case into the room, looking for somewhere to put it, when without warning the handle broke, and the heavy case crashed to the ground. The cord that secured it snapped, and the sides split wide open, spilling out a pile of brand new Bibles.

I shall never forget the expression on Brother V's face.

His cheeks flushed, wide-eyed, two shocks of matted hair clinging to his sweat-covered forehead, his hand hanging down. Not a single word came from him.

Then his expression changed and he moved towards me, arms outstretched.

'Ah, Bibles,' he sighed, supporting himself on my arms. His wife, startled by the noise of the falling suitcase, was still rooted to the spot. They looked at the heap of Bibles, and I looked at them.

'Oh, brother, what a treasure you have brought into our house!' His voice was almost drowned in tears—he was so overwhelmed with happiness and gratitude.

His wife still stood as if petrified, gazing at the pile of Bibles in the middle of the room.

PART THREE

Bulgaria

1

My Bible is confiscated

IN 1968 the autumn seemed reluctant to give way to
winter. The summer holidays had raced by and were
almost over when I realised that I had done hardly anything; so I decided to take the days off that were still due
to me at Christmas.

It was late autumn when I received a letter from Bulgaria—an urgent invitation from a Christian whom I had
met before to visit him at the seaside resort of Varna.

The year was nearly at its end; yet the soft and gentle
autumn weather seemed to encourage acceptance. I hesitated. Was it advisable to go to Varna in the winter?

I read the letter again. The urgency of the invitation
impressed itself upon me, and I began to make plans. I
weighed up my chances of obtaining a passport, reckoned
up the financial outlay involved and how much free time
I had at my disposal. Strangely, everything seemed
favourable. I came to the conclusion that God's hand was
in it.

There was not much of a queue at the police station
next morning. After all, not many people spent their
winter holidays abroad. How would the authorities react
to my proposal to visit the seaside in the middle of
winter? My heart began to sink, but I still felt something
urging me on. So I found the application papers and
began to fill them in.

At the passport office window a man with an oval face
took the completed papers and read through them,
underlining the word 'Bulgaria' twice.

'Just a visit, is that right?'

'That's right,' I mumbled.

'Varna is your destination?'

I was rather embarrassed, but the man did not seem to care too much what my reaction was.

'Please sign here.'

I signed.

Outside a cool wind sprang up, and snow clouds began to scud past. It looked as if winter had decided to come at last. Not holiday weather. I stopped and for a few minutes thought of going back, telling them I'd changed my mind and wasn't going . . .

There was a stronger gust, which seemed to go through my body. I wrapped my overcoat more tightly round me.

'Lord,' I sighed, 'please show me what your will is.' I consoled myself with the thought that if it were not the Lord's will, he would prevent me from obtaining a passport—but something told me I was going to Bulgaria again.

The wind was now blowing hard against my back as I made my way to the tram stop. No tram came. People were passing me all the time, hurrying home. A familiar sense of unease began to dominate me.

Suddenly someone called out, and I spun round to see an old friend, hurrying in my direction.

'Where have you been all these years?' he greeted me.

'And where have you got to, Alex?' I responded. I would have forgotten my problems if he had not suddenly asked me, 'Where are you off to?'

'I've just been to the police station.'

'Going abroad?'

'Why not?' I replied with a smile, slapping him on the shoulder.

'Going far? New Year's party?'

'No. Not far. Just across the border.'

'Bulgaria?'

'Yes, Varna.'

'Ha, ha!' He broke into a laugh that shook his whole body. 'So you miss the beaches, do you? Ha, ha, ha! The weather looks just right.'

I stood there in silence, taken aback by this unexpected attitude. 'I'm going for a very important reason, Alex,' I informed him.

'Consul or ambassador?' he laughed. Everything about him seemed to be dissolved in laughter—his eyes, his cheeks, his mouth. By now I was extremely annoyed, and tried to change the subject.

'More important than either. Anyway, what are you doing in these parts?'

'Yes, I can't imagine you being without serious problems,' he went on, and, at last controlling his laughter, reeled off a list of his own family problems and financial difficulties. At last his tram came, and he climbed in, waving goodbye.

I stayed behind, still waiting. Everyone seemed to be laughing at me. I remembered a man who had looked over my shoulder as I filled in the application form: he had seemed amused. So had the clerk at the passport desk. And now my friend!

My thoughts gave me no peace. Was it just me, or was the devil trying to hinder a work that would be to the honour and glory of God? Was it really God's will for me to go? What would I find to do in Varna? What if it was all snowed up?

'Lord, Lord,' I prayed. 'Show me if it really is your will.'

Still trembling with cold and nervousness, I waited for God to answer. And I vowed I would tell no one else if I did eventually decide to go to Bulgaria.

The arrival of the tram interrupted my thoughts. Back at the office other problems got the upper hand.

Time seemed to rush by. Autumn finally changed to winter. Then one day I came home late from work and saw the postman at my house. My heart beat a little faster. Could this be the letter? The envelope had the police insignia on it, and I tore it open eagerly. In a few days, I read, my passport would be ready.

Happiness mingled once more with uneasiness. There were now only three days to Christmas: should I go this year or next year? Outside, the endless rain fell, monotonous and cold. I fell on my knees again. 'Lord, lead me to do only what is your will.'

After that I could breathe much more easily. All the heaviness and anxiety was lifted from my chest, and now I knew: it was definitely right for me to go—as soon as possible.

The preparations for my departure were as usual very slight. A small suitcase, a few changes of clothes, some cold food, presents for the family to which I was going, and my indispensable pocket Bible. I always travelled light—but I always had enough.

At dawn on the day after Christmas I set out for Sofia. I was a mixture of happiness and trepidation; there is always uneasiness when you do not know exactly where you are going, or why, but I had a conviction that what I was doing was according to the will of God.

As the train gathered speed, I stood looking out of the window, humming to myself and watching the telegraph poles flash by. Different places, bare trees, constantly changing countryside. Within the next few hours I would discover why God was sending me to Varna.

At the frontier the train jolted to a halt, and the border guards came to check my passport. After looking under the seats in the compartment one turned to me and asked, 'Have you any weapons?'

'I am unarmed, comrade,' I replied with a smile.

A few moments later, two customs officers appeared. There were no other passengers in the compartment, and this privacy had many advantages—I had been able to sing and pray, and do all that I wanted. To be alone is often advantageous for God's children—they are in the presence of God, heaven and themselves. They have the privilege of reflection, of dialogue with God and fellowship with heaven.

'Good morning.' The customs officer saluted with a wry smile.

'May it be a good one,' I replied pleasantly.

'What are you taking into Bulgaria?' asked his colleague coldly.

'Nothing in particular. Just some small presents.'

86

'Kindly open your luggage.' He gave me a piercing look, apparently intended to intimidate me. He felt along the inside edge of the suitcase and then, still unsatisfied, turned everything upside down with one movement of his hand. A rectangular packet, wrapped in paper, came to the surface, and he quickly grabbed it.

'What have you got there, comrade?'

'A book.'

He undid the white paper and tried to make out the title of the book, reading it syllable by syllable.

'The Bible ... or ... Holy Scripture.' He looked at me questioningly. 'You are not allowed to cross the border with something like this,' he said, visibly irritated.

'Why not?'

'You don't ask questions like that round here. Orders are orders. Do you understand?'

'I understand, but ... this is a book which never leaves my side. Just as some people like to take other books to read on a journey, I take a Bible with me. And where is the law, comrade, which says I am not allowed to take my own Bible across the frontier?'

I knew very well that there was no such law. Having a Bible was permissible. It was obtaining one from outside that was forbidden.

'What is your profession?' asked the other officer, interrupting his colleague in an effort to calm the atmosphere, and taking the Bible into his own hands.

I told him. A government post.

'Really? And you read books like that?'

'Of course. A bit every day.'

'And what do you find so interesting about this book?' he inquired, fascinated to find a person like myself reading the Bible.

'Do you know,' I said, addressing both of them, 'that this book, which you believe is a bunch of fairy tales, contains the entire history of mankind? In it you can find out about man's past, present and future.'

'Don't start on all that nonsense,' said the first officer sharply.

'More than that,' I continued, 'it includes the life and destiny of all men, including you.'

'That's incredible. Fancy an intelligent and cultured man like yourself reading and believing all those fairy tales!'

'It is written here, for instance, that you are sinful men, that the wages of sin is death, and that the only way to escape this death is to believe in the Lord Jesus Christ, who died for the sins of all men.'

They were looking at me intently. They were surprised, and apparently eager to listen.

'The Bible tells us that the Lord Jesus loved tax collectors. Your colleague Matthew was even called to leave his job and follow the Lord.'

'Look,' said the first officer to his colleague, 'this fellow is preaching at us the day after Christmas. That's enough of those fairy tales.'

'I let you speak, but you've gone too far,' agreed the other man, taking the Bible and cramming it into his briefcase.

'Please let me have my Bible,' I said. 'I need it.'

'To go and preach to other people? Is that the game?'

'I have never been without my Bible. Please let me have it back.'

'Stop pleading. You don't argue here. I can see you're not used to crossing frontiers.'

'Take me to your chief. There's no law that prohibits a person from having a Bible on him when he crosses the frontier.'

'Law or no law, you will do as we say. Do you want to be put off the train?' He took out his book of receipts for goods impounded at the frontier, and I fell silent. I knew that what they said went, and there was nothing I could do. I regretted having to part with the Bible, but I was glad that I had been able to witness for the Lord in front of men who were so closed to the gospel.

The taller of the two men asked for my passport, then slowly copied down my name, noted 'The Bible or Holy Scripture', signed the form, tore it out and handed it to me.

'When you return, present this form at our office, and you will get your book back.'

I didn't reply. A smile of satisfaction broadened over his face. 'We shall see you again,' said the other officer as the door slid shut. It was not long before the train was moving again.

How difficult it was to accept the will and plan of God without knowing the reason behind it. Why had he allowed my Bible to be taken? I knew that in the end there must be a reason.

The train streaked on, devouring the distance. The fields were deserted, and the snowless landscape blended with the sky. Everything seemed dull and a leaden grey. A pale sun, like a tiny gold coin, rolled slowly across a trembling sky. I felt an emptiness inside me.

The train was very late arriving in Varna, and to my great disappointment there was no one waiting for me. I had no idea where to go. The address on the envelope was anything but clear—the street was there, followed by something that looked like a G, and that was all I could decipher. People were streaming past me left and right.

I stopped a passer by, who just shrugged his shoulders nonchalantly and looked at me pityingly. I showed him the envelope, but he could not make head or tail of the address, although he came from Varna. Another directed me towards a taxi-rank. One of the drivers there looked me up and down, then tried in vain to decipher the address. For some reason he grew annoyed, raised his voice and handed the paper back abruptly.

As I stood there feeling completely lost, a bus drew up. Instinctively I boarded it. When the conductor asked me where I wanted to go, I showed him the envelope, but he could not make it out either.

A young man who had been following the exchange came over, paid my fare and, racking his brains, endeavoured to remember a few words of Romanian. He spoke to a few other passengers, then looked for a long time at the address on the envelope. At last he gave me some directions.

After about twelve minutes the young man signalled to me to get off the bus with him. It was drizzling, and the streets were almost deserted. We crossed the road, went round a corner and then down a narrow tarred street, lined on both sides with rows of birch trees. At the first intersection my guide stopped and, putting his hand on my shoulder, pointed vaguely, gesticulated wildly and spoke to me in a mixture of Romanian and Bulgarian. He was sorry he could not be of more help, he said—then went back the way we had come.

I stood alone in the rain. Streets turned off in all directions; which way should I go? Not knowing what to do, I stared ahead, and suddenly my eyes became blurred. 'Lord, at your bidding and in your name have I come here. I beg and plead with you: please guide me,' I prayed fervently. Then it seemed that a shudder went through my body.

In the distance I heard footsteps coming rapidly towards me. I went on praying, and the steps became louder. Someone was getting very close. As I stepped to the edge of the pavement to let him pass I heard a voice say in apparently perfect Romanian, 'Go straight ahead and knock on the high gate, the one worn with age.'

Startled, I looked up, but there was no one there. The street was empty, except for the rain. I could still hear the footsteps, but this time they were moving away.

I stood as if turned to stone, until I realised that the rain was beginning to soak into me. I set off down the street.

Occasionally I looked over my shoulder, hoping to see someone, but I was quite alone. The street started to go uphill slightly, and the pavement became narrower. The rain was coming down harder, and the cold began to eat into me. Then suddenly in front of me was a gate—large, high, its paint peeling with age. I knocked hard, but there was no reply. I knocked again.

There was a grating sound as a blind was drawn. The window screeched slowly up, and the head of a woman with dishevelled, copper-coloured hair appeared.

'Does Mr — live here?' I asked, naming the man who had written to me.

The woman brushed aside one or two wisps of hair and pushed them behind her ears. She indicated that I would have to go through the courtyard, and that the person I was looking for lived at the other end of it.

So I had come to exactly the right address. I could hardly believe it. Without a shadow of doubt, it was God who had guided me.

As I entered the courtyard I could hardly contain my excitement. In front of me appeared a low house which seemed almost to be built into the fence. The courtyard was deserted, and I approached the door gingerly.

It was opened by a robust man with a round face. As soon as he saw me he flung his arms round my neck, then, taking me by the shoulders, drew me inside. He was radiant with joy. As he looked at me he kept repeating, 'Praise the Lord.'

After I had refreshed myself with a short sleep, during which my host's wife returned from work and the child from school, we spent a long time speaking about the way in which God was working in both our countries. Time flew by. That evening there was to be a meeting at the church; so we got ready and left.

The muddy road climbed the hills on the outskirts of the town. It was raining intermittently, and the ground was very slippery; from time to time I had to steady myself by grabbing hold of wayside bushes. It was as black as pitch, and I had trouble following my friend. As if to apologise for the difficulties of the road, he related the history of the little church in the area.

The old buildings in which they used to meet had been taken from them; now they had to move around, and meet where they could. Many pastors, he said, had been dismissed and replaced by men faithful to the state—some of them were even informers.

'Why didn't you protest?' I asked.

'Do you think anyone would have listened? No one would have taken any notice. They say they have no time for things like that.'

Both of us fell silent. This was nothing new; we were both concerned about the future of Christians and their places of worship. When we reached the top of the hill, there appeared in front of us a small, fragile old house, half hidden behind a group of trees. From two windows a pale light shone out feebly.

'This is where we worship,' whispered my friend. He stopped me and pointed to the town, spread out below. 'Down there, in the main street, where the brightest lights are, we once used to have our meeting hall.'

We stood in silence for a moment. Then my friend added, 'But praise the Lord for everything. He has called us to patient endurance. Tomorrow or the day after we shall not be able to meet here any more.'

The place in which these Christians now met, so far as I could gather, had until quite recently been deserted. The room in which they gathered was not very large, but the chairs were neatly arranged, there were some fine panels with Bible texts on them, and a tiny pulpit hung with a dark blue velvet cloth created an intimate but reverent atmosphere. The cloth was embroidered in gold with a cross and the words, 'God is Love'.

We were very conscious of God's presence. In the dimness of the room the tired, worn-out faces of the worshippers glowed with an air of happiness—a happiness that brightened even those faces most marked with age. When my friend stood up and introduced me, then invited me to speak from the pulpit, all seemed to be going well.

A young girl student with russet hair came up to translate for me. After passing on the traditional greetings I read slowly, in broken Bulgarian, the verse that was embroidered on the pulpit cloth.

'More than everything else, God is love. This I have experienced even from childhood, and I can sense and see concrete examples of it today. God is not in the first place vengeance or a devouring fire. God is in the first place love. What we see on the cross of Golgotha is not an indication of the authority, vengeance or almighty power of God. It is the supreme indication of his supreme love.

'Jesus Christ came into the world as the complete expression of divine love. The Father loves us so much that he sent his only Son for our redemption. Jesus loved us so much that he gave his own life in direct payment for our sins. What links us with each other, and all of us with heaven, is love.'

As we made our way home down the hillside, squeezing between bushes and avoiding puddles, the chimes of the cathedral rang out midnight, setting up a strangely powerful echo that resounded across the valley.

2

Singing on the cliffs

THE NEXT day I got up early. I was tempted as so often
to turn over, close my eyes and remain in that enchanted
state somewhere between dream and reality, but there was
a commotion in the next room, and the door opened
slightly. My host's little boy poked his pudgy face gingerly through the gap. When he saw that I was not asleep
he dived on to my bed, arms outstretched like a goal-
keeper making a dramatic save.

For breakfast we ate Bulgarian pancakes, then together
the boy and I hurried along to the corner of the street,
which was bathed in the gentle light of a late December
sun. Half dragging me, he led me through the town and
out in the direction of the sea.

The rows of wave-crests, bathed in silvery-yellow light,
stretched into the far distance. Shells of every shape and
description covered the beach. We played games with the
waves until our clothes were covered with water and
sand. Then we climbed the cliff, and with our jackets
slung over our shoulders wandered contentedly along the
cliff-top, singing.

The boy knew the words in Bulgarian, and I told him
what they were in Romanian: 'O Lord my God, when I
in awesome wonder consider all the worlds thy hands
have made . . .'

The boy looked at me, his big eyes like black almonds.
He tried to pronounce the Romanian words one by one,
struggling with the sounds until he had memorised them.

The day was warm, and there were many people
out walking on the cliff-top. I began to hum another
hymn, and the young lad listened attentively, taking up a
position in front of me so as to catch every note. Then he
stopped me, and with a smile waved both hands furiously

above his head; he wanted me to sing at full volume. I smiled and hugged him.

'Am I allowed to do that?' I asked.

When he had understood me, he remained thoughtful for a moment, and then indicated that as far as I was concerned, it was all right. Nobody would understand Romanian. So I asked him if he would like to sing with me in Bulgarian.

He shook his head and, speaking softly and quickly, tried to explain. I caught the word 'politics'. It wasn't hard to understand what he meant.

'It's no good,' he said, shaking his head slowly. But it would be all right in a foreign language . . .

I have never been able to sing very well, but at his insistence I began one of my native hymns. He encouraged me with clenched fists to sing louder and louder, humming and clapping in support. From time to time a young couple would stop to listen, or a woman with a pram, or a small group of young men. Others turned their heads as they walked past. They seemed to like the singing.

At last we sat down on a bench. By now I had stopped my musical efforts and was watching the seagulls diving into the silver water. The boy stood dutifully beside me, apparently also lost in thought. Suddenly he turned towards me.

'When you come to our house again,' he said slowly, 'I will ask my father to buy me a guitar, and then we can both walk along the cliff singing.'

'Good,' I said. 'Why don't you come with your father? He can sing and accompany himself on the guitar.'

He raised his piercing eyes and looked at me fixedly. 'Daddy,' he said . . . and made signs to indicate that his father was afraid to do so.

As we strolled back along the beach he again tried to tell me something. He repeated the word 'Daddy', and a shudder went through his body. Finally I understood that a friend of his father's had either sung or prayed somewhere, and his father had afterwards had trouble with the police.

Back at the house, the unease and sadness must have registered on my face. The boy noticed it.

'Why are you sad? Has someone been beating you up?' he asked.

'No,' I replied in Bulgarian, nodding my head emphatically in the Bulgarian manner to make my meaning plain. 'Has someone been beaten up here?'

He shook his head in the affirmative.

'Who?'

'A Christian in the town.'

'How do you know?'

'I heard Dad speaking to Mother about it. They beat him up badly . . . blood flowed . . . He was taken to hospital. He was twisted with pain.'

'But why?'

Then he told me, with the help of gestures, the story from the beginning. How a friend of his father's who often came round to his house, and with whom he often used to play, had been bruised and battered by the police. The whole account was illustrated so freely with gestures that I had little difficulty in deciphering the meaning.

'Why?' I repeated.

The boy went over to his father's cupboard and took out a familiar book. He showed it to me.

'Bibles . . . many Bibles,' he said.

3

A sack full of Bibles

AT MEAL time my host tried to make it clear to me that I should not speak to any of the neighbours or give the appearance that I was a foreigner. I could see that he was rather disturbed, and his uneasiness began to rub off on me. He began to talk again in a whisper, while his wife busied herself with something out in the yard.

Today you must take a rest. If you like, we can go out and see the town in the evening, because tomorrow, when I return from work, we will be going to another area altogether. A friend of mine needs your help.'

'Who is this friend?'

'You'll see. You'll meet him.' He was getting more and more uneasy, and so was I. After a pause he went on, 'I . . . er . . . know nothing about all this . . . I have never met you. You are on your own now. After we leave this place, as far as you are concerned, I don't know you until you arrive home safely in Romania. After that . . . you can write me—but discreetly, you understand, so that no one will be any the wiser.'

He paused, apparently satisfied with the way he had put things.

'You know, I . . . we . . . er . . . I'm not the man you're looking for. I'm not cut out for this sort of work.'

He looked up at me again, and I was rather embarrassed. I shifted my eyes to the table, examining the cracks in minute detail. His hands, also on the table, were trembling.

'What's the trouble?' I asked.

Brother G coughed, and shook his head. 'I'll have nothing more to do with it. I've finished my mission. As far as I'm concerned, I've never met you.' He paused. 'This kind of thing is just not for me. I'm happy to go to church from time to time, sit down next to my wife and children, maybe even give a short message occasionally—and then go home . . . without any fuss . . .'

He stopped short. His wife was still busy in the yard outside. Inside, only the ticking of the clock interrupted the silence.

'Yes, brother,' said my host at last, 'tomorrow I'll take you to see the town, and then . . .'

'And then?'

'We'll have to go our separate ways. You can do much more than I can. I've got a wife and child . . .'

'Good,' I said. 'I don't want to cause you any problems. I am grateful to you for all that you've done. May the Lord bless you.'

'Yes, yes. Of course, no one will know about what we have discussed. As far as we are concerned, you just came to Varna for a holiday—or if you prefer, you haven't been here at all.' He looked at me questioningly.

'Don't worry. It'll be all right' I replied. 'The Lord will protect us to the end—and even if he doesn't, we'll still do all that we can for him, won't we?'

'Yes, I believe that,' he said. 'I believe that.' After another pause, he added, 'You see, I'm almost like an official and after all, we have to be subject to the authorities, as the Lord teaches in his Word. I believe it is good to live in peace with all men . . . My wife and I are very weak when it comes to suffering . . . I don't think we are called to that.'

The next day we left for Burgas. The weather was fine; the sun was shining, and a gentle breeze stirred the branches of the trees. I became more and more intrigued by the precautions that my companion took, and I began to wonder again, as I prayed silently, just what God's purpose was in bringing me to Bulgaria.

As the car drove on, the shadows began to lengthen across the road. At Burgas the street lights were already on, and we entered the town with considerable caution.

My companion's anxiety and my own lack of comprehension, of which he was well aware, put a barrier between us. The moment was fast approaching when we would have to say goodbye, but we still had to find the address. In a dark side-street he stopped the car in the shadow of a spreading tree.

He described to me the man we had to meet, and with whom I was to deal. It sounded like someone I knew—a young, slightly built man with brown hair—and this relieved my anxiety somewhat.

We left the car and proceeded in silence, keeping in the shadow of the trees. After we had turned a corner to the right, my companion stopped suddenly and turned to me.

'I can't go any further with you. I can't see too clearly, and won't be able to make out which is the right building. I can't . . . I shouldn't have got mixed up in this in the first place. But the Lord knows all things, and he will keep us. I'm just not cut out for this sort of work. Do as you think best. Remember—you don't know me.'

He spoke more and more nervously, looking round him all the time. When he saw someone coming he withdrew completely into the shadow. I too began to feel a little afraid.

'Tell me what the trouble is, brother,' I urged him.

'I'm not going any further. Up the street you will see on your left a courtyard in which there is a very bright light—that's the meeting place.' He explained that I would have to enter as cautiously as possible and sit near the back of the room. After the service I should go out with the first ones to reach the door, and go up to Brother B without anyone noticing . . .

He took me by the shoulders and turned me in the right direction.

'Look, over there, next to that lamp-post—that's where you must go. I can't come any further.'

'I understand, I understand,' I answered him. He looked thoughtful for a moment, then stepped aside. In a flash he was gone.

According to my watch the service would soon be over. I would have to hurry. But everything in my head was spinning, and it seemed to be getting darker and darker.

Bowing my head, I murmured as slowly as I could, 'Lord, I do not believe you have brought me here to be lost. I have come to do your will. I beg you to direct me. Please open my eyes.'

The street was very dark. I passed many courtyards with lamps in them, but none fitted the description I had been given. At the top of the street I stopped. The seconds ticked by.

Suddenly a sensation like an electric current seemed to go through me. I stood rooted to the spot, and my mouth seemed to open of its own accord. 'Lord, it's in your name that I came here!'

Then something seemed to impel me forwards, and I walked briskly on. Suddenly, however, my steps became abnormally heavy, and I stopped—in front of a narrow courtyard, lit only by a street lamp burning at half power. Now I understood. This was the place.

Putting my suitcase down in a dark corner near the door, I crept into the meeting. No one saw me, except perhaps the preacher. And the man I was looking for was sitting directly in front of me!

As they came out of the meeting I stepped up to him and gripped his arm. Astonished to see me, he looked round nervously and made his way over to the shadow of a wall, signalling me to follow. When we were some way away from the others, he walked past me, whispering as he did so, 'Follow me.'

He made his way through the group of worshippers and out on to the street, holding his child by the hand and discussing something in a quiet voice with his wife. I followed at a distance for some time, then suddenly they vanished. I couldn't work out where they had gone, and was looking desperately around me when a man who had been walking on the other side of the street crossed over. As he passed me, he whispered, 'It's the tall house on the right. There's a narrow entrance at the back. Second floor, Flat 23.' He disappeared behind a pile of bricks on a building site.

The house was only about ten yards further on.

After groping around in the dark, I found the entrance

and began to climb the twisting, unlit staircase. I tapped my way up, feeling the wall, and then each step as I came to it, until I found the floor I was looking for. The door opened slowly.

The brother took me by the shoulders and led me inside, cautioning me; in the flat next door lived someone who had been assigned by the secret police to keep an eye on him. I tiptoed gingerly into the dining-room.

Both of us fell on our knees. We knew nothing much about each other, but we felt that the love of God united us, and we prayed fervently together, asking God to protect us and lead us further—but above all thanking him. As we prayed we could see that we were entirely of like mind, that we had the same desires and the same spirit in us—the Spirit of the Lord Jesus Christ.

Everything about the house, every object seemed to warm to me, to smile at me and bid me welcome, just as my host had. The loving Christian atmosphere rejoiced my soul. I felt completely at home.

Soon the door opened slowly, and a short man edged his way in. He was carrying a large sack on his back. He put it down in the middle of the room, and leaned against the table to get his breath back.

'It's heavy—very heavy. It's been a heavy day today.'

He gave a deep sigh, and his eyes began to sparkle strangely. He eyed me closely from head to foot. Then he stretched out his hand, told me his name, embraced me and sat down. With this man, too, I felt an immediate bond. The spirit often speaks at a deeper level than the word, so that, as by a magnet, one is instinctively either attracted or repelled.

I looked at the canvas sack. It must contain something heavy—and judging by the uneven shapes, I saw it must be books. As I talked my eyes kept returning to the sack. My host noticed, stretched out his hand and gripped the bottom of it, pulling hard. Out of it tumbled—books, with black covers.

'Bibles! Bibles!' I exclaimed, swooping down and taking up two copies, one of them wrapped in fine rice paper. 'Where did you get them?'

'From the Lord, brother.'

'How beautiful they are.'

'Even more beautiful than Bulgarian Bibles . . . ' His eyes shone like suns. Almost without realising it we found ourselves embracing one another, while the sack slipped further open to disgorge more of its contents. I could see why the police had someone watching this family!

'Thank you, dear heavenly Father,' my host broke out spontaneously, 'that you have answered my prayer, so that I can now understand your plan.' His voice grew more intense and powerful, and tears streamed down his cheeks. He seemed to be speaking to someone very near.

I opened my eyes a little to look at his face. It was glowing, but the skin was covered with bluish-red blotches and scars. I wondered what he had been through.

4

Those who share in Christ's sufferings

I FELT as if I had known my new friends for years. As we talked, the expression on my host's face radiated happiness. I looked again at the violet blotches on his neck, extending to beneath his open shirt, and the expression on my own face darkened. He noticed.

'I was arrested by the police,' he explained, pointing to the marks. 'The "official" Christians helped them. Be on your guard against them. You can never tell who is a stranger among us—who is the Judas disguised, the wolf in sheep's clothing. Beware of them—beware of them at all costs. The authorities have even infiltrated party members. Some of them have been baptised.'

He spoke in short bursts, every word seeming to demand a great effort. His chest was heaving and his face was pale.

'Was this recently?' I ventured.

'A few days ago. Someone brought me some Bibles. I distributed some, and there was a complaint. I was taken to the secret police. They kept me there for three days. For three days and three nights they beat me up—using hands, feet, rubber truncheons and I don't know what else—anything they could lay their hands on. They beat me until neither they nor I could stand up any more.'

'What were they after?'

'They wanted to know where I'd got the Bibles. Who had given them to me, and where I had distributed them. You realise ...' (he whispered in my ear) '... that I couldn't tell them. How could I give away brothers who had risked their lives to bring us the Word, and how could I reveal who I had given them to?

'I refused to say a word, and this infuriated them; so

they laid into me all the more. They are completely merciless—men without heart.'

His eyes were dim with tears, but as I looked into them I could discern a mysterious glow. I gazed at him with admiration and not without some envy. Here was a man who had had a share in Christ's sufferings.

'After three days and three nights of beatings, they brought me back home in a car at night. I was as bloated as a barrel. My family could hardly recognise me; my head was badly cut and my body covered with bruises. For a whole week my wife and children kept me wrapped in sheets and gave me cold compresses until I recovered. Now I feel much better, praise the Lord.'

'Praise the Lord,' I repeated.

'It is to him alone that I owe the fact that I am still alive. And now my one desire is to work without ceasing for him and for his kingdom. I haven't much longer to work before the Lord comes. I want him to find me working for him.

'You know, sufferings always strengthen us. It is as we suffer misfortune for his sake that we realise how near he is.'

So there are still martyrs to be found today, I thought. But he seemed to read my mind.

'No,' he said. 'The sufferings of the present are nothing, compared with the glory that is to come.'

I began to understand. Behind bars, behind the curtains that separate us from one another, over there in that great unknown there are Christians fashioned of gold, shining martyrs who may be called upon at any moment to pay with their lives for their witness to Christ.

I thanked the Lord for sending me to this house. I was now sure that he was going to bless me over and above my expectations. In spite of the fact that my host still bore signs of his beating, that his bruises were still very painful, and that I was a witness of all this, neither of us was in the least afraid.

It was a moving atmosphere, warm and filled with heavenly love. We sensed that the Lord was looking down on us. We knelt, one on either side of the sack, and began to pray. It was rather an unusual prayer—like the torrent that breaks out suddenly when the snows of winter melt in spring. With our tired hands resting on the sack of Bibles, we were no longer masters of the words we uttered, or of the ideas in our minds. It was as if all that remained of me was a prayer of the soul and spirit.

We rose from our knees, tired yet full of happiness, our spirits joined together in perfect unity in the Lord. My friend remained thoughtful for a moment. Neither of us wanted to break the spell. Then he smiled at me and whispered, 'How are you going to take them?'

'I don't know.'

'But you will take them, won't you?'

'Of course,' I said. 'I've got no choice.'

I began to pack the Bibles, at first into my small suitcase, but it held only a few. The rest went haphazardly into a canvas bag.

'Are you going to take them just like that?' asked my host.

'Yes.'

He shook his head and remained pensive.

'I'm not taking them; it's the Lord who's taking them,' I added.

He bent down and picked up the luggage. 'But it's heavy. How will you carry it?'

'I'm young and strong,' I laughed.

'I'm afraid I can't help you. You know how it is—I'm always followed. It would be dangerous for you.'

'There's no need to help me. God will watch over and protect me.'

He patted me on the shoulder. 'That is the sort of child that God needs.'

'Yes, that is the sort,' I echoed his words, stretching out my hand.

The luggage was now ready, all the Bibles packed in. It seems to me now sheer madness to have attempted to cross, of all borders, the one between Bulgaria and Romania—where the customs officials always take their time and look at everything in detail—with all those Bibles so haphazardly packed. But at the time it didn't seem to be a problem at all. It was just as if I was going to make a normal journey from one town to another. At that moment I had more faith in God than at any time in my life that I can remember.

I lay down on the bed—not to go to sleep, because there was no time, but to be alone for a few moments with God. Before the first rays of dawn came and people began to move about on the streets I would have to leave for the station to deposit my luggage.

The train wasn't due to leave until evening; so I had the day to myself. But we both felt I should avoid all contact with other Christians. So, once free of my luggage, I strolled into the town. A gentle but chilly wind was blowing in from the sea.

Towards mid-day I came by accident to the sea-front. There is a strange attraction about water stretching to infinity; when I saw the shiny blue glinting through the trees I felt a deep satisfaction. The beach was empty, except for the shells that glistened like pearls in the intermittent sun. I walked along the wet sand. Great waves came roaring in from the open sea, bursting and crashing one after the other, strewing shells in their wake. I relaxed, and watched.

Suddenly, as if brought in by the waves and deposited on the sand in front of me, I saw the sack of Bibles. It began to grow to an enormous size and assume the shape of a tall tree with a huge trunk, dwarfing me completely. I felt my soul twitch with pain.

'How will you take them across? . . . They'll catch you on the border . . . Bibles . . . You don't really need to do it.' The deep, clear, authoritarian voice came from somewhere behind me, and I started and looked round. There was no one to be seen. A shudder cut right through me, and I cried out as loudly as I could, 'The Lord rebuke you, Satan. You liar! Get out of here!'

My whole body was unbearably tense, then I suddenly went limp, like a bowstring after the arrow has been fired. I ran quickly up the beach, as if free of a terrible strain.

I climbed the cliff and started to walk slowly along it, enjoying the soft rays of the sun on my face. The voice I had heard continued to ring in my ears—sometimes cajoling, sometimes offering advice, sometimes threatening. I began to pray inwardly, but I still could not get any peace. Fear began to grip me more tightly. I stiffened, trying to overcome it.

Then I saw a bench in the sun. The lack of sleep the previous night, the nervous strain and the walk in the town had begun to tell on me, and I lay down on the bench, resting my head on my hands. I closed my eyes to avoid the glare of the sun's rays reflecting off the water. I dozed off to sleep—or so it appeared.

I found myself on the edge of clear blue water, so transparent that it looked like glass. I stood there spellbound by the water reflecting the rays of a sun I could not see. My gaze shifted to the horizon, which seemed to blend with the sky in an infinity of blue. All at once I saw what seemed to be a large placard, white as snow. It was as wide as the whole horizon, like a gigantic curtain whose folds were dancing in the wind.

It was the movement which first caught my attention; then I noticed some large letters. I tried in vain to read them, because the movement of the folds prevented me—the letters appeared and disappeared, melting into one another. I was bitterly disappointed.

Then on my right I heard a voice saying, 'I have come to help you.'

I couldn't see anyone. 'Lord, what is written there?' I asked.

'I am the Lord God who has been with you up till now, and who will see you through to the end.'

It was a deep, powerful voice, so loud that it seemed to shake everything, like a crack of thunder echoing endlessly into the distance.

I quivered as if something had stung me. I opened my eyes and turned round abruptly, but there was not a soul to be seen, except in the distance two children playing in the sun. The sea seemed to boom as heavily as ever. But the words kept echoing through my brain:

'I am the Lord your God.'

5

New Year's Eve at the frontier

WITH SOME difficulty, and with the help of a kindly Bulgarian, I succeeded in hauling my luggage up into the carriage and on to the rack. We were the only travellers in the compartment, and my companion made several attempts to engage me in conversation. Each time I was unable to catch what he was saying, and eventually he gave up, began to look out of the window, and at last fell asleep.

As the train gathered speed I listened to the rhythmic clatter of the wheels and was startled now and again by a cluster of lights that flashed past the window.

I tried to get to sleep, but couldn't. The frontier crossing began to loom ominously large, and a shiver of fear went through me. I began to wonder whether I could arrange my luggage more carefully, so that it would not be obvious that there were books inside. Perhaps it would be possible to hide some of them elsewhere?

It occurred to me for some reason that it would be better to put the bag which contained the Bibles behind the suitcase, and stand the suitcase upright. So I stood up slowly, taking care not to disturb my fellow-passenger, and started to reach for the rack. Then I changed my mind. The holdall with the Bibles was much bigger than my tiny suitcase.

Then a new problem; the carriage in which we were travelling was, we were told, not going any further than the border. This meant a move to another carriage as soon as possible, and it was going to be sheer agony, carrying the heavy cases all the way. What if someone asked what was in them? There were a thousand horrible possibilities.

However, there was no time to lose. In a few minutes

we would be in Rusé, the border town, and that was where the customs men got on.

I felt the train slowing down as I dragged the luggage to the door. A Bulgarian helped me down with my luggage on to the platform. 'Books?' he mumbled, as he handed me down the case. I shut up like a clam. If he could tell what I was carrying in the bag, the customs men certainly wouldn't have any difficulty.

The night was black as pitch; there was not a breath of wind, and frost was in the air. I made my way along the platform, with some difficulty, to the one second-class carriage bound for Romania.

Suitcases were lying round everywhere. I went from compartment to compartment, but nowhere could I find a space. The thought of having to remain in the corridor with my luggage, exposed to the eyes of the customs officials, sent a fresh shiver down my spine.

Suddenly, a voice hailed me: 'Halloooo.'

I turned in surprise. An old acquaintance was beckoning to me above the heads of the crowds cramming the corridor; there was still a free seat next to him. I was amazed. Only a few minutes before I had gone through the compartments without being able to find a single seat.

Next to the window an elderly man was asleep. With his dark complexion he had to be a Bulgarian. Near the door were two men who could not have been more different from one another. The elder of the two was white-haired, with a swarthy complexion, and as thin as a rake. He was puffing at a pipe so long that it seemed to hang down his chest like a tie. Opposite him sat an enormous young fellow, as tall as he was wide. His hair was blond, and he had huge arms. He didn't look far off thirty stone.

Above him on the luggage rack was a vast trunk. It would have been almost comic if he had had anything smaller. As I entered the compartment they were in the middle of a heated discussion; when I realised they were father and son, I was astounded.

When the giant saw me come in, he got up and shifted

his enormous trunk a bit further down the rack, to make room for my cases. My friend and I were able to hoist my heavy holdall up to the height of the rack, but when the giant saw that our strength was sorely taxed, he jumped up and flicked the case into position next to his own. I paused to get my breath back, thanked him and wedged myself in beside my friend.

The man with the pipe looked at us closely, then exchanged a few remarks in Norwegian with the giant. They then returned to the heated discussion that I had interrupted.

'You seem to have a lot of books in that case,' my friend remarked.

'Yes, I do have some books,' I replied casually. 'What did you manage to buy in Bulgaria?'

'Oh, just little things, you know—er, and a leather coat. I hope the customs don't make a fuss.' He glanced anxiously up at the luggage rack. At the end of the corridor I could hear the commotion and bustle as the Bulgarian customs officers started to work their way down the carriage. Panicking suddenly, I closed my eyes to pray. But almost immediately my friend nudged me.

'Are you going to sleep? Can't you hear the customs men coming?'

I looked round. It seemed to me to be Satan's doing that at the very moment I wanted to pray I was prevented from doing so.

'Aren't you afraid of the customs?' my friend persisted. 'I suppose the books don't pose a problem for you.'

I didn't reply, but closed my eyes again and began to pray; and as I did so I heard a powerful voice in my right ear. It was the same one I had heard on the beach.

'Now they'll get you. Why do you have to take all those Bibles anyway?'

I opened my eyes with a start. The same people were still in the compartment. A stony, nervous silence reigned.

'No, no,' I screamed inwardly. 'You, Lord, have promised to see me right through to the end. I am convinced that you will. Glory to you for endless ages! Get out,

Satan, you liar. Get out!' My whole being began to over-flow in a prayer to God. A terrible battle was taking place within me.

All the time the customs men were coming nearer and nearer. I was seized with a feeling of nausea. When the door was thrown abruptly open, and the two uniformed men appeared, I felt as if my heart was being pierced with a needle.

The short man was the first to be asked to take down his suitcase. Inside were toys and objects of folk art—commercial samples.

The bag containing the Bibles stood there on the luggage rack, staring the customs men in the eyes. Its curious shape was bound to attract attention. I glanced discreetly up at it, then the open case in front of me, then at the customs men as they worked their way unhurriedly through it. I clenched my fists, then dug my fingers down behind the seat covering. As I looked up at my case, some words from the Bible came into my mind.

'Have I not told you that if you believe you will see the glory of God?'

Where did those words come from? What did they refer to? I forgot about the customs men, the luggage and everything else, searching my mind for the answers. It was a complete blank.

Then, like a flash, I came to my senses. The Lord was speaking to me. It was he who was saying it. I had only to believe; nothing could happen to me.

'Declaration please!' The customs officer turned in my direction, and my friend gave me a nudge in the ribs. The officer looked at our two declarations, stamped them and asked us the usual question.

'What are you bringing back from Bulgaria?'

'Just odds and ends,' said my friend.

'Please take that suitcase down.'

Trembling slightly, my friend pulled his case down and unlocked it with shaking hands. The officer took out sev-eral objects one by one, to look at them more closely. Underneath a sheet of thin paper the sleeves of a leather coat were visible. The other officer began to pull it out.

'We can't let that through,' said the first officer.

'You'll have to pay duty on it,' added the other, in comically broken Romanian.

The two Norwegians looked at each other questioningly. The Bulgarian next to me gazed in stupefaction, while I glanced up at my own luggage, fighting to control myself, then looking at the leather coat and putting on an apathetic expression. I gritted my teeth so hard that I was afraid I was going to break them.

The customs officers continued to haggle. In the end one of them said: 'Either you pay, or we confiscate it.'

The other glanced up and seemed to be looking right at my luggage. I froze. But he continued the discussion with my friend, holding in one hand the leather coat. As they couldn't understand one another properly, both the customs officers went out, followed by my friend.

It was as if a lump of ice had suddenly melted and fallen off my chest. I could breathe freely again—for the moment.

The door opened, and my friend returned, a happy look on his face.

'I diddled them on that one,' he said; 'now if I can persuade our customs that I don't have to pay, I'm as good as home and dry.'

My own luggage had not been touched: I felt a surge of joy. For a few moments I forgot that I would soon have to face the Romanian customs.

'They didn't look in your things, did they?' my friend asked suddenly.

'What is there to look for? I haven't any leather coats, that's for sure,' I joked.

'Don't they know that it's New Year's Eve? Can't they leave us in peace for a change?' he complained.

'Orders are orders. What can they do about it?'

'I suppose so,' he sighed, then added: 'Perhaps the Romanians have gone off somewhere to celebrate, and we'll get off cheaply. Eh? What do you say to that? You and your books—aren't you worried about them?'

Silence descended again. I was lost in my own world,

giving thanks to the Lord, and praying for fresh help with the next problem: the Romanian customs.

With a rattle, the door of the compartment was pulled back again, and two men in immaculate uniforms saluted us politely. I was the first to hand in a declaration.

'As far as I can see,' the customs officer said looking at the form, 'you have nothing to declare.'

'That's the way it should be,' I replied. 'Travel light with no clutter, and avoid all the unnecessary fuss and bother. I know,' I added, plucking up courage, 'that it only causes inconvenience for you if we don't. I never have any problems.'

'That's very good,' he replied. 'But not everyone thinks like you. Many travel abroad just to make a quick profit. Others bring all sorts of forbidden objects back, and illegal material. Some even dare to bring in prohibited books. You know, there are all sorts of sects . . .' He broke off to glance up at the luggage rack, on which stood my case containing the Bibles.

'Well I never,' I put in quickly. 'Is that possible?'

'Yes, it's quite true. These sects,' he continued, 'are full of fanatics. Religion, and weeds like that, are still flourishing.' He squeezed on to the seat beside me, to give his colleague more room for manoeuvre.

'Really?' I said in surprise. 'What about all those books, all those atheistic lectures, the radio and TV broadcasts? Haven't they destroyed all that?'

'Destroyed it? I can see you haven't been initiated into these problems.' He leaned closer and dropped his voice. 'Some days ago I saw a book called "The Funny Bible" in a shop window. Out of curiosity I leafed through it. It was utter rubbish. Half of it was just quotations from the Bible, and the other half consisted of fairy tales that not even a child would believe today.'

'I haven't read it. You say it's not very good?'

'It certainly isn't. Even funnier are those who have published it.'

'Yes, but surely Lenin said, religion is doomed to disappear,' I continued, trying to keep the conversation going.

'Nothing of the kind. The struggle is as futile as ever, because you see, man will always remain man. His ideal is a happy life without any problems, with no wants. Only religion, a fanatical faith, can give him that.'

'Look at the size of that trunk,' said the second customs officer, interrupting us. We all looked towards the giant's enormous trunk, while the officer next to me got to his feet.

The two Norwegians were amused, and chatted to one another in their own language. They evidently found the feverish activity of the customs men very funny, and seemed very relaxed and at ease. From time to time they glanced at their watches, surprised that the train had not yet begun to move.

'No, there's nothing here,' said the man who was carrying out the search. He turned to the short man, who continued to puff unperturbed at his pipe, and said in German, 'Thank you.'

I closed my eyes and leaned my head back, pretending to be asleep. My heart was beating abnormally fast. Every fibre in my body, every muscle was tensed to the maximum. Then I remembered the way God had protected me the last time I had crossed this frontier, and someone seemed to whisper in my ear: 'I am today the same Lord.' A pleasant warmth came over me.

The voices of the officials, the click of suitcases being opened and closed, seemed far off in the distance. I had the impression that I was no longer in the carriage, but floating somewhere in space. It was as if I were watching a play being performed. My friend took down his suitcase and then put it back again, and it all seemed like a dream. Then a strange voice jolted me out of my reverie.

'Goodbye, and have a pleasant journey.' Just as he was going out of the door the customs officer turned round to me and stretched out his hand. 'Goodbye. It's been nice meeting you. If ever you come this way again, know that you have a friend at the customs. I'll put in a good word for you.'

'And I've been glad to meet you,' I said.

I could hardly bring myself to accept the fact that they had left. After a short while doubts began to creep in again. A strange voice seemed to whisper in my ear: 'Perhaps they'll come back again; perhaps they smell a rat and will come back. You won't get off as easily as that.'

I went into the corridor, and stood staring out of the window. In the distance the first rays of dawn began to emerge from behind the black streaks on the horizon. I pulled open the window. The dawn seemed to symbolise the victory of light over darkness. Gradually, the darkness was banished to the uttermost ends of the heavens.

Then, suddenly, I remembered my Bible. I went back quickly into the compartment, looked among my papers and found the receipt I had been given when I entered Bulgaria.

I hesitated. Should I go and claim it? What if they remembered they hadn't checked my luggage? What was the point in worrying about one Bible, when I now had so many—and new ones at that? Perhaps the Lord wanted them to keep the Bible so that one of them could read it and come to a knowledge of salvation.

I decided to leave things as they were—but I had no peace. Who was I to leave Bibles lying around? They were precious. Didn't I need it? People risked their necks to bring Bibles to Romania—didn't I realise how much they were in demand? And this was the one I'd taken everywhere—full of my own notes.

I was in a dilemma—but in the end I made up my mind to try and get the Bible back. While the officer who had been talking to me was occupied I would give the receipt to the other, and tell him I had an object that had been confiscated.

So I went along the corridor, following the customs men at a discreet distance. But wherever one of them went, the other stuck to him like a leech. I could see no possibility of getting my Bible back, yet something kept urging me on.

As they came to the last compartment and went in, the one I wanted to see paused in the corridor to look through the window at something that had caught his attention. I hurried up to him, and showed him my receipt.

He read it slowly, syllable by syllable: 'The Bi-ble or Ho-ly Scrip-ture'. Then he stared at me to fix my face in his memory.

'I'll bring it to you in your compartment when we've finished here.'

Just what I had feared would happen. He was going to come and search my baggage, and he would find the Bibles. What I had grasped with one hand, I had lost with the other.

'Lord, forgive my thoughtless action,' I prayed. 'You can see that I have no understanding. Only you can save me. I depend entirely on you and your goodness. Don't leave me in the lurch, now that I'm so nearly home.'

My heart was pounding like a hammer. I was like water that had been poured out and could not be gathered up and put back into the well.

My friend came and stood beside me. 'Simply fantastic,' he said, slapping me on the back.

'No I'm not,' I exclaimed.

'What are you saying? That's the second time the customs men have looked in the direction of your luggage and haven't seen a thing.'

'I don't think so.'

'But didn't you notice? They just did not see your cases. Don't you understand? You know all the luggage they went through—they even looked under the seats. But no one troubled you, or said anything to you.'

'Perhaps,' I murmured.

'Perhaps you have a friend who works at the customs. Is that how it is? Have you got some good contacts? I noticed the officer sat down and had a chat with you.'

'Yes, I do have connections. I know a high-up person.'

'There, what did I tell you? I can see you're telling the truth now. Why didn't you say so to begin with? That explains everything.'

'Yes, he's a very important person.'

'On this side of the border, or both sides?'

'For all customs men—and everyone else,' I said with a smile. He shook his head in amazement.

'That's the way to travel. You can take what you want when you know no one's going to search your luggage.'

'That's right,' I said, rather wishing that he would leave me in peace for a while. Then a voice in my ear—'What about the Bible?'—made me jump.

'What's the matter?' asked my friend.

'Nothing. I've remembered they did search my case on my way out of the country, and impounded something.'

'Then go and ask them for it. Why get worked up over such a little thing? Remember, you've got a high-up friend. As far as I can see, he's probably issued an order that you should be left alone this time.'

'Yes, that is possible,' I replied, a little embarrassed.

'But then again,' he continued, looking at me closely, 'perhaps they will remember that they haven't checked your luggage. But if you have friends in high places, you have no need to worry.'

I was flabbergasted. He had guessed my anxieties exactly, and he could see I was nervous. He took me by the shoulders and said in a friendly tone: 'Why all this worry? Your friend will protect you, even if they take all your luggage away.'

'Yes,' I said. 'You know, you're right. He has protected me up to now, and he'll go on protecting me.'

'Well, don't wait until the train leaves. Go and claim the impounded object now. What right have they to keep it? I'd make a bit of fuss if I were you. Let them know who's boss.'

'That's true,' I thought. At any moment the train could leave. I hurried down the train, and saw the customs men get out and disappear round the back of the customs buildings. I started to run. The signal for the train to leave was already being given. Round the corner, they saw me coming.

'What do you want?'

'You've got . . .'

'Didn't I tell you to wait?'

'I'm sorry. I was afraid the train would leave.'

'It won't leave till we're ready.'

Sheepishly, I returned to my seat.

'How did you get on?' asked my companion.

'They're going to bring it to me here.'

The minutes dragged by. Every noise made me jump. At last I heard someone calling my name, and one of the customs men came in.

'Sign this receipt, please,' he said, and smiled. 'We're not as bad as you think!'

'I didn't say that,' I replied. 'You've treated me very well.'

'Well,' he smiled, 'we don't often meet people who can see our side of it.' And he took my Bible from his bag and gave it to me.

Within a few minutes the train was on its way. My companion kept looking at me, then leaned closer.

'What's the matter?' he asked. 'You're different. Your face has changed completely.'

I shrugged my shoulders, but he kept looking at me. I knew that I *was* completely changed, but I couldn't explain it—except as a miracle.

We were approaching Bucharest when my friend broke the silence. 'I would like to get to know your "helper" . . . I'm planning a trip to Yugoslavia; perhaps we could go together.'

'I'll introduce you to my helper,' I said. 'You need him.'

'Is he waiting for you at the station?'

'No, he's in the train.'

'Well, introduce me to him now,' he said enthusiastically.

'No, not yet.'

He rubbed his hands in anticipation and kept glancing at me as the train neared its destination. When we got out, I heard him calling me as I was looking for a porter to help with my luggage.

'Have you forgotten?' he asked.

'No,' I said. 'But I've got to take care of my luggage.' I gave it to a porter, then took my companion aside.

'My helper is Jesus,' I told him.

'Are you joking?'

'No, never. My friend—my helper—is Christ. Everything you've seen has been done by him, and him alone. You can get to know him by reading this book.' I handed him a New Testament.

He looked at me, speechless. Then he came closer. 'I thought only God could have helped you like that. Are you a Christian?'

'Yes. And you must become one too.'

'I . . . I teach people there is no God,' he said. 'I must earn my living, you understand—but I know he does exist, and today I saw him with my own eyes.'

'You need to know him,' I repeated.

6

Witness on a train

I PORED over the map for a long time as I planned my journey. Was I going to the right place? Was the Lord really leading me? Then I made up my mind.

I have always liked travelling, and I considered it a real happinesss to 'travel in Bibles'. Can there be a greater blessing than to bring food to the starving with one's own hands?

I had forgotten it was Saturday. The station was very crowded. Long queues were waiting for tickets, and I was worried that the train would leave before I could reach it. I even thought this might be a sign that I should not go. But I joined the end of the queue.

Everything seemed to happen excruciatingly slowly, as I counted the minutes. At last I got my ticket and dashed over to the left-luggage office, hearing as I went the loud-speakers announce the imminent departure of my train.

'Please hurry. My train's due to leave,' I shouted at the left-luggage counter.

'Why didn't you get here sooner?'

He picked up my suitcase.

'What on earth have you got in it? I nearly broke my back.'

I snatched the case and made off quickly as a whistle sounded. The train had started to move when I reached the end carriage and sprang on to the running board.

I stood in the corridor to get my breath back. Though relieved to catch the train, I was unable to suppress that nagging doubt whether I was doing the right thing. Inwardly, I cried out for a confirming sign from God.

There was quite a crush in the corridor, but in the first compartment a seat appeared to be free, so I took it. After a few moments the ticket collector came in. I held out my ticket, then suddenly realised that this train had only reserved seats on it.

'I saw this empty seat,' I said, 'but if it is reserved I'll vacate it.'

He looked surprised. 'But this is your seat. Number 24, carriage 16.' He held the ticket next to the space marked on the seating list, as if to convince me. I was astounded. My prayer had already been answered.

The journey proved very tiring. In the silent compartment a suffocating heat permeated everywhere. Eventually I dozed off.

'What's the time?' A voice addressed the fat man sitting next to me.

'Nine,' he answered curtly, annoyed at being disturbed.

'How time flies,' I said.

The fat man rubbed his eyes and nodded.

'A day goes past—a week, a year, and . . . a life,' I went on.

'That's right,' sighed a grey-haired man. 'It seems only yesterday that I was a young man like you. The years have come and gone.'

'And tomorrow I shall be as you are.'

'I've been through difficult times,' he said. 'Two terrible world wars—I even fought in the first one. It seems just like yesterday.'

'Today is past, and tomorrow is not yet here—they are just names that disappear.'

'That's how God meant it to be,' said a plump woman in a red head-scarf.

'Yes, we are so transitory, just like a vapour,' I said, looking at my watch. I would soon be leaving the train. 'And yet in this life that is so short and transitory, we can attain eternity.'

The old man gave me an intent look. The lady nodded her head. An old man on the other side of the compartment wiped his forehead. I could see they were all waiting for me to go on.

'You can all find a place in paradise—not only in the future life, but here and now.'

'That's a lot to claim,' said the old man.

'It certainly is,' I agreed. 'Our life on earth is so short. Soon we have to leave—we have no choice in the matter. The question is, where do we go? What have we achieved? Have we made sure of our future in eternity?'

I paused. The train had begun to reduce speed. In the corridor people were collecting their luggage together.

'For our sinful world—for every one of us, even though we're all full of sin—God the Father sent his Son, Jesus Christ, to die in our place, paying for all our sins. Through him we can have forgiveness.'

Already people had begun to get off the train. But I knew that it was due to stop here for a few minutes.

'The essential thing is to believe in Jesus Christ.'

I began to take down my suitcase. No one said a word. I could see they wanted me to continue, but time was running out. I took some tracts from my pocket and began to distribute them.

'Let me have one.'

'Me too.'

'I'd like one.'

I went out into the corridor. People there had seen I'd been giving something out in the compartment and held out their hands. I distributed all that I had, then left the train. As I made my way to the station exit, the train began to move.

Darkness covered everything. A few lights blinked faintly like tired eyes as I struggled along the narrow street with my heavy suitcase, imagining the joy of my fellow-Christians as they received the Bibles. I felt very small and inadequate beside the need of those who were eagerly awaiting my arrival. I was like a dwarf trying to move a mountain.

The silence around me was broken only occasionally by some night bird, or the barking of a dog. From some way off I could see a light flickering in the window of the house I was heading for, and was relieved that the occupants had obviously not yet retired.

The gate was still open, and I wondered why. Perhaps

they had guests. I stopped short of the door and deliberated, finally deciding to leave the suitcase hidden somewhere in the garden and to enter the house empty-handed.

I had to knock twice before I heard the sound of footsteps. The key turned in the lock, and a middle-aged man appeared in the doorway.

'Ah,' he said with a broad smile. 'There you are. Lena, that's why we didn't go to bed earlier!' He drew me inside. It was a warm and intimate atmosphere, and I felt immediately at home. Smiling, his wife came quickly to greet me.

'How much longer are you going to go charging round the countryside before you realise that there are lambs here to feed?' she asked.

When I brought the suitcase into the house, Brother J could tell from its weight why I had come.

'May the Lord be praised,' he said. 'No one else seems to think of coming to us. There are no Bibles, no hymn-books, nothing here. But look how the Lord has heard our prayers.' He was rubbing his hands like an eager child.

When I opened the case he stood there with mouth agape and eyes wide. Then he raised his hands to heaven and burst out, 'Lord, I thank you that you have answered our prayers. I felt that it would not be long.'

His wife stood rooted to the spot. 'What a treasure,' she said. 'May the Lord bless you.'

'In that suitcase,' said Brother J, 'I can see the seed that will bring fruit in this area to God's glory. It is difficult; people are steeped in tradition, still a bit backward ... But the Lord has called us to work here.

'You see, if there's nothing to read—if a man can't read something direct from the Bible, he will not be very likely to believe what you say. In many villages they say they've never even heard of the Bible. Where they have, it's just a book the priest reads—a holy book.'

'Are there really villages where people haven't heard of the Word of God?' I asked.

'How little you know our region,' he smiled. 'I can see

you'll have to stay with us a bit longer. A few days ago there was a man here from one of the villages—he was in the army with me. I asked him if he'd read anything from the Bible, and he said, "What's that?" And he's a man who has read some books, and has his wits about him.'

For some time neither of us spoke. Then he added, 'Without weapons it is difficult to fight. You can speak to a man as much as you like and witness to him about the Lord—tell him about salvation—but if he reads it himself, in the Bible, he can go home and confirm for himself what you've been saying.'

'And what if I give you all these Bibles?'

'If you do, may the Lord bless you. Then we shall be without excuse before God and man.'

'Do the Christians themselves have enough Bibles?'

He laughed. 'You're asking the sort of question I'd expect from someone who'd just stepped off the plane from America. It would be more to the point to ask if the preachers had enough to go round!'

He kept gazing at the Bibles. At last he blurted out, 'Are they all for us?'

'Well . . .' I hesitated, 'there aren't too many Christians in this area . . .'

'Not many? There are a lot more than you think. Besides, people are beginning to take an interest in spiritual things. And the more people hear about the Bible, the more they'll want one for themselves.

'Thousands are needed for Christians who've been praying for one for years. Then there are the tens of thousands who are all ready to receive the Lord . . . Every year hundreds are converted. How are they going to grow if they have nothing to read?'

The discussion went on far into the night. Before I went to bed, I said, 'I'm convinced the Lord is stretching out his hand to help you. If I had the quantities you're looking for, I wouldn't hesitate.'

'Just give us Bibles,' he said, 'and we'll cover whole regions for the Lord.'

7

Casting out a demon

AT THE slightest breath of wind, leaves rained down from the trees. We walked in silence past empty fields. Both Brother J and myself were deep in thought.

'It is very dry,' he said heavily.

'Dry in the earth and in the soul,' I responded.

'That's right,' he agreed. 'But it's going to rain in this region soon—an immense stream of blessings from God. We're praying and waiting.'

'You'll have to work for it, brother. There is no other way. If you love this region, put a lot of work into it. Don't wait for others to come. You're here for a reason.'

'We believe that, but there are difficulties. It's Bibles we need—and a lot of them.'

The road had turned to the right, down towards a small village.

'Here there are few Christians,' he said, 'but they are very keen. None of them has a Bible. One has a New Testament, which is as old as the hills—half the Gospel of Matthew is missing. They take turns to read it. In two weeks it goes round everyone, then returns to the eldest of them. It might be a good idea to give him a large Bible, because he can't see very well . . .'

'All right. You know the situation better than I do.'

'But I'll take the New Testament,' he continued thoughtfully, 'and give it to someone else—someone younger. What do you think?'

'Do as the Lord tells you—what seems best. As long as you're not biased . . .'

We took a little street on the left and knocked on a door. The man we had come to see was about to leave for a prayer meeting. Tears of astonishment and pleasure came to his eyes as we greeted him.

'This is the man,' said my companion, 'who since he has come to faith in Christ never refuses anyone anything. Some made fun of him, refusing to return money and other things they'd borrowed, but he just kept on giving, in the name of the Lord.'

'Yes, brother,' he said in a soft voice. 'The Lord said, "Give to him that asks you."'

Brother J reached under his coat and brought out a large Bible, with black cover and red edging. He held it out to the old man, who stood there completely at a loss, looking first at me, then at my companion, then at the Bible.

'Take it, brother,' urged my friend.

He stretched out his hand shyly to touch the Bible, then looked at me again.

'I never thought I'd hold a new Bible in my hands,' he marvelled. 'I've never read a Bible which had all its pages intact. Now I can read it from morning to evening.' He stopped short, his eyes filled with tears. 'Where did you get it?'

'From the Lord.'

'And whom should I pay and thank for this? It's you, sir, I think,' he said, turning to me.

'No,' I said, stepping back. 'It's the Lord—him alone. You have only to thank the Lord, and all those who have sacrificed their possessions so that this book could be printed and brought here.'

'Yes, yes. Thank you,' he said. 'But I don't even know who you are. Where are you from?'

'It's better if you don't know.'

He pressed the Bible tighter and tighter to his chest, as if afraid that someone would take it from him. Then he rushed towards me and hugged me as hard as he could, without saying a word.

I couldn't get the old man out of my mind. 'How many more like him do you think there are?' I asked my friend.

'Very many. And the young people have an even greater need. It's incredible. The educated young people come to us illiterates and ask us what the Bible says about various things. They ask us to read the Bible to them, because they've heard about it, and want to know. If only we could give them Bibles.'

'Do you have a preaching permit?'

'Permit? The Lord Jesus told us to preach the gospel. Who can stop us? Just give us Bibles.'

It was the same problem, I thought. The same need everywhere. Thousands of hands, and no Bibles to fill them.

My companion was looking at me. 'You have seen just one case,' he said, 'and it has made you think. How do you think we feel when we see it every day?'

I didn't reply.

We managed to get hold of a second-hand car, and so reached the next village fairly quickly.

'Let's go to where they meet for prayer,' suggested my companion. 'The Christians here have been fasting for three days. Let's go and pray with them. I want to thank the Lord for what you've brought me.'

That day the prayer meeting was in a house almost hidden behind a hill to the north of the village. When we arrived I could see the place was full of people on their knees, praying continuously to God. The simplicity of it impressed me. I thought of the catacombs. Hanging on one wall was a large panel with the text 'We preach Christ, and him crucified'. The opposite wall was bare.

To the right, in front of me, a twenty-five-year-old woman was sitting on a chair. Her hair was dishevelled and her dress was torn; her face was drawn, and saliva trickled from the corner of her mouth. She was bound to two men on either side of her, one of whom was much younger than the other, who had white hair. The first man, I learned, was her husband, and the other was her father. The woman was possessed by a demon.

They had all come together to pray for her healing. Soon after we arrived they stopped, and sang a hymn.

Then a tall red-haired man with shining eyes approached the woman, who became agitated. The two men on either side of her tried to calm her. Another man brought a vial of oil, and she began to struggle fiercely. But he seemed used to it. The woman muttered something and then screamed, but the two men on each side of her put their hands over her mouth. The man with the oil said something soothing, but she tried even harder to fight free. The crowd began to stir, and people strained forward to see. Then I heard the calm but firm voice of the older man who had brought the oil.

'My brothers, and those listening to us. The case we have before us is not something to which we are totally unaccustomed, for in the Bible we read of many people who had unclean spirits.'

'Aaaah!' the woman burst out. Some people at the back got to their feet.

'Do not be afraid,' he continued. 'We know that Jesus Christ had power and authority over unclean spirits when he was on earth, and he still has it now that he is in heaven. The apostle James teaches us that those who are ill should be anointed with oil, that we should pray for them and they will be healed.

'We have absolute faith in what is written. We know that God respects his Word. So we are only doing what the Lord has commanded us to do; we shall anoint the sick person in the name of the Lord, and we shall pray.'

As if at a signal the whole assembly stood up, and I could no longer see. I assumed that the old man was anointing the woman. There was a deep silence as some of the men laid hands on her, and then I heard again the loud voice of the old man.

'We thank you that you hear our prayers. We thank you that you heal the sick. Thank you that you have heard our cries. We thank you.'

After a pause, the same powerful voice again.

'In the name of Jesus Christ, I command you, unclean spirit, to leave this person and to depart into the desert!'

There was a loud crack, and the woman fell to the

ground, screaming and uttering unintelligible sounds. The whole room shook, and something like a current of air seemed to pass through the open window.

Then I saw the woman sprawled on the ground between two benches. She was lying on her right side with her face to the ground, and from her mouth there came a sort of yellow froth. There was a deathly pallor on her face, and there were scarcely any signs of life.

Her eyes seemed far away, and she lay there motionless, her dress even more badly torn. Beside her her father and husband stood, deeply worried, not knowing what to believe. They looked at each other, then at the woman. The father started towards her, but the old man restrained him.

'Let her calm down and revive. There were many demons inside her, but now she is free. Praise the Lord.'

Someone said, 'Let's sing a hymn,' and soon it was echoing powerfully through the house. The woman revived little by little. Her face began to regain its colour, her eyes became brighter, and her breathing returned to normal. She started, as if she had been abruptly roused from a dream. She tried to get up, but fell back again and remained quite still for a while.

Her face continued to brighten, and her eyes regained their lustre. Underneath the bench there was a pool of foam. The woman grew more and more anxious as she realised what had happened to her.

After a while she tried to sit up again. She was still not strong enough, but the two men stretched out their hands and helped her on to the bench. The crowd was still tense. The woman's father made a large sign of the cross. The husband's cheeks were flushed as he kept looking at his wife.

They sang another hymn, and the old man with white hair, apparently the leader of the assembly, made his way slowly to the pulpit. He gazed at the crowd intently.

'What you have seen here is not our work,' he said. 'We are by ourselves powerless against such forces. We just pray, and God does everything. Glory be to him for all eternity. Our God is the same God he has always been.

He performs miracles just as he did two thousand years ago. The God in whom we put our trust is a God of miracles.

'It is this God who has shown himself to us today by freeing this woman of a host of unclean spirits. He is the God who calls you to repentance.'

He paused, as if to gain new strength. I looked at the small, frail old man and wondered where he got his power.

'This woman has been delivered from unclean spirits before your eyes, so that you might witness the power of God and believe in him. As you can all see, she is now well, and serves as witness to the fact that God can heal anyone today. Is anyone here ill? Let him come with full assurance and faith to Jesus Christ.

'The Lord Jesus never turned anyone away. He received all who came to him, in whatever state they were—lepers, cripples, dumb, deaf or possessed by demons, as this woman was, who is known to all of you. In the past he received them; it is the same today.'

He paused to clear his throat, then continued, 'Come to me all ye that labour and are overburdened, and I will give you rest for your souls. These are the words of the Lord Jesus. All we are doing is to repeat his call.'

His voice rang out as insistently as ever, and with full authority. As soon as he stopped, there was a commotion at the back of the room. People were moving around. Gradually men and women with eyes full of tears made their way to the front, and the space in front of the improvised pulpit was soon crammed. The preacher stood there motionless, eyes lowered, wrinkled cheeks quivering.

A strange calm spread. The faces of all present were radiant with excitement and happiness.

The woman had meanwhile recovered, and someone had put a sweater over her shoulders. The full force of what had happened had not yet struck her: Her hair was still dishevelled, but her eyes had regained their brightness. She now sat much closer to her husband, who continued gazing at her with wide eyes and a gentle smile.

A woman prayed, 'I thank you that you have delivered this woman from the power of unclean spirits.'

And the woman who had been possessed burst into tears. 'Thank you for having mercy on me,' she prayed.

Everyone else grew quiet. The woman was speaking normally, but poured out her heart in prayer, and the leader remained silent, allowing her to continue her prayer of thanksgiving. At last she covered her face with her hands and wept uncontrollably.

Then the leader prayed for those who had come forward, and for those who were ill. 'Continue to manifest yourself in our midst through signs and miracles, and we shall continue to praise you for all that you give us,' he concluded.

With that the meeting closed. The woman now sat calmly on the bench, apparently deep in thought. Many people came closer as if to convince themselves that the woman had been completely cured. They filed past her, thanking God when they saw that she was really well again, and then made for the door. Then the old preacher came up to her.

'May the Lord be praised,' he said. 'Isn't his mercy great?'

'Wonderful,' she replied.

'How do you feel?'

'I don't quite know how to describe it. It's like a deep peace.' She smiled. 'I feel well—very well, brother.'

'May the Lord be praised! He has delivered you. He will receive you and forgive you if you are prepared to be faithful to him.'

'I want to serve him all my life. I shall never forget the wonderful things he has done for me.'

Gradually, the room emptied. The young man rose to his feet, looked at his wife and took her by the arm. 'Let's go home, my dear,' he said gently.

In the courtyard outside people were still talking about what had happened. I had been watching the events so closely that I hadn't noticed my host slip out. Seeing me alone, the old preacher came up to me.

'I hope you don't mind my asking, but where are you from?'

'A long way away,' I replied.

He hesitated. 'Good, good, brother. Will you be staying here long?'

'No. I shall be leaving in a few moments.'

At that moment my companion reappeared and took me to one side. 'I'm sorry to have left you on your own. Everything is all right. There's just one more visit I'd like to make.'

We walked along in silence, but quickly. Apparently there was some way to go. The clouds grew darker as we walked.

'Is it much further?' I asked, looking anxiously at the sky.

'Just a bit further. We'll get there before the rain comes on.'

After a few minutes we entered a long, narrow court-yard, at the end of which was a small house with lemon-coloured walls. My companion went on ahead and knocked. An elderly man answered, and the two greeted each other.

'Is your wife at home?'

'Please come in.'

Lowering our heads to avoid the beam, we entered the house. A woman of about sixty-five was tidying up hur-riedly.

'May the peace of the Lord be with you,' my com-panion greeted her. 'Do you feel better?'

She replied that she did, and the old man motioned us to take a seat. But my friend was in no hurry to sit down; I could see that he did not intend to stay long. I was impatient to see why we had come, for I was sure that all the Bibles had been distributed at the service, though I had seen nothing. To visit an old man wasn't a bad thing to do, I mused—in fact it was a Christian duty.

'Sister A,' he said. 'Have you ever read anything from the Bible?'

'Of course I have. Our brothers are always on time; every eleven days they bring me the Bible to read. I read it all day, because we're getting old and there's not much work to do.

'But my husband still doesn't believe that everything in the Bible is true. He even said that if the Lord really answered prayers he would answer my prayer—because I have been praying for a Bible. What an idea!' She looked fondly at her husband, who was still smiling silently. It was obvious he knew my companion fairly well.

'So it's like that, is it?' asked Brother J.

'That's right. If it's true that he answers prayer, and my wife receives a Bible, I'll believe as you do, and I'll join you,' he said with an air of finality.

'All right. Don't forget the Lord heard when you made that promise.' Then, turning to the wife, Brother J asked her, 'How many years have you been praying for a Bible?'

'About seven.'

'And you still haven't given up hope? Do you still believe the Lord can send you one?'

'Yes. I've never given up. I believe with all my heart, but perhaps it's not time yet. As you know, the Lord's time is not our idea of time.'

The old man interrupted. 'I don't really believe,' he said, 'but the other day something—I don't know what—made me think she'd be getting the book soon. I don't say the Lord doesn't answer prayer, but to get your prayers answered you'd have to be a saint.'

'Do you know something,' said Brother J. 'I don't think it will be long before you get a Bible.'

The old couple looked at us closely. For a few moments there was silence. My companion looked at me, then thrust his hand into his pocket and drew out a large, new, shining Bible. No one spoke for a while.

Then my friend said, 'Here's the Bible, Sister A. It has come direct from God. He has granted your request after seven years.'

The old man stared, wide-eyed. So did his wife, who took the Bible, clasped it to her breast and kissed it, as if it were priceless treasure. Her eyes welled up with tears. Then she turned to her husband and, scarcely able to contain her joy, burst out, 'now tell me that God doesn't answer prayer!'

After the old man had recovered slightly from his astonishment, he said, 'What more is there to say? I can see it with my own eyes. All I have to do now is repent.'

We left, in a hurry to catch the bus. The clouds were still threatening, and I felt the first drops of rain on my cheeks.

PART FOUR

Romania

1

Rendezvous in the mountains

THE CAR in which I was preparing to leave was large and spacious. What was more, it was black, which had several advantages; for instance, people would think that a large car of that colour must belong to an important person. Of course, it would not pass unnoticed, but I considered that a minor problem. I had a lot of luggage; so a big car was essential anyway.

A long journey lay ahead; I planned to visit quite a wide area. And I had a fellow-traveller—the only man who would be able to take over from me in an emergency.

'How does that look?' I asked him.

'Good,' he murmured, somewhat sleepily, then added, 'Mainly because I'm sure we're surrounded by guardian angels.'

As the time of our departure approached, I became more and more nervous. I knew I was carrying treasure—God's Word—and I knew I would meet two kinds of people: those who would receive Bibles thankfully, and those who could not stand the sight of them.

There in a courtyard behind a red-brick wall, on the grass where the dew glistened in the dawn, we knelt in the presence of God. First we thanked him for the car, and for all that we had in it, and then we sought his help for the journey. When we rose I felt an inward peace which I saw as confirmation that our prayers had been heard. We climbed into the car.

To start with, my friend took the wheel. The streets were still empty, and we hurried to get out of town before the heavy traffic got going. From a narrow, winding street we emerged on to the main road. The car was running well.

We had a lot of work to do that day. I prayed silently as we drove along, and my friend noticed this.

'What's the matter?' he asked.

'Nothing,' I replied.

'Then let's sing.' And he began to sing in his high-pitched voice—closer to a soprano than a tenor.

Later, I began to explain about the first rendezvous, and he repeated my instructions.

'Dead right,' I congratulated him. 'As for the rest, watch me.'

'Of course.'

The sun was shining straight in through the windscreen as we entered the town. We found the rendezvous point without much difficulty, but we were a little late. I ran quickly round the corner to where our contact was—rather impatiently—waiting.

'Where have you been?' he asked.

I took the empty sack that he was carrying, and as we walked along I said, 'Stay here. When you hear the noise of a car driving off round the corner, you will find the sack underneath that tree.' I pointed.

'Be careful. Never be tempted to sell any of the Bibles. Give them first to preachers, then to those in greatest need. Any that are left should go to families with many children.'

He held me back, as I made to leave. 'Brother, how can I thank you?'

'Thank the Lord. Peace be with you.'

In a few minutes everything was ready. I placed the full sack at the foot of the tree and left. After we had gone a short distance we slowed down, and I saw in the mirror a man emerge, take the sack and disappear.

'Praise the Lord,' said my friend, rubbing his hands in satisfaction.

Silence descended on us once again. Both of us kept our eyes on the road, which wound up into the hills and descended again into valleys. The atmosphere was very close, and in the car the heat was overpowering; so we opened the windows. From time to time, we sang a hymn.

We came to the brow of a rounded hill, from where the countryside stretched out on both sides below us. We were approaching the mountains—but before we could cross them we had a stop to make—this time in a village, which posed additional problems.

The hole in the road caused the car to pitch and roll, and from time to time there was a loud grating sound. I decided it would be prudent to slow down, even though we were in a hurry. Then the road improved again, and we left great clouds of dust in our wake as we sped along.

We hurtled through a village, the few people who were around turning their heads as we went past. We had a rendezvous at the next village. As we came into the country again I began to recognise the area—right, past a maize field, turn up again at the wood ... 'Stop here.'

The field was empty. There was no one in sight.

'Keep a sharp look out,' I warned, and set off through the field. The maize was tall, and the heat overpowering. The sharp leaves cut my hands, face and throat, but I had to go on. I quickened my step and eventually emerged from the field at the meeting place. No one there, and it was already late. I stood wondering whether it was worth waiting. I looked round carefully. There was no one in sight.

Then I had an idea. I began to whistle a hymn, at the same time glancing round for any movement in the maize. Suddenly, to my right, just ten yards ahead of me, the maize parted—to reveal a man's head. I called out, giving the customary greeting, but there was no reply. I did not know what to think.

Then two men appeared, one younger and shorter than the other. They came towards me, whispering. I didn't recognise them, which no doubt accounted for their strange behaviour.

'Peace be with you,' I said, holding out my hand. But they went on whispering, not sure whether I was their man.

'Peace be with you,' I repeated. 'Where are your sacks?'

'Here,' they replied together.

'Come with me. Have you been waiting long?'

'Oh, that's all right. We reckoned on you being late. It's such a bad road,' said the younger man, more at ease.

'It wasn't too bad. Has everything gone well so far?'

'Praise the Lord, yes.'

We walked back in silence through the field, with the tall crop slowing us down, and the sharp leaves beating against our faces. The heat was incredible, and the rows of maize seemed unending. I watched the two men out of the corner of my eye. They looked frightened, I thought—not used to this sort of thing. The younger walked ahead, while the other stayed level with me, deep in thought. At last we reached the road, and the young man looked anxiously round.

A lorry, travelling at some speed, was coming towards us, trailing a great pall of dust. We crossed the road quickly and made for the car, which was parked away from the road. There my friend was waiting impatiently. We opened the boot and, without saying a word, began to fill the two sacks.

'What beautiful Bibles!' exclaimed the young man.

'I praise you, Lord,' mumured the other, holding one tightly to his chest. 'You will never guess how many years we have been waiting for these, and how many tears we have shed for them.'

Then he tried to thank me, but I would not let him. 'Thank the Lord instead,' I told him. 'For those villages in the hills.'

'Yes,' he said. 'Everything is more difficult in the mountains.'

I prepared to leave, but the younger man restrained me. 'If we should fine someone who has had an old Bible for years, how much should we sell him a new one for?'

'For as much as it cost you to buy it.'

He looked crestfallen. As I started the car, I remembered something else. 'As far as you are concerned, you haven't seen me, or this car. Agreed? Give my greetings to Brother G!'

'Don't worry,' said the older man.

'Even if they string me up,' added the younger.

In the distance I heard the rattle of another lorry approaching. I could see as it passed that there were a few men inside, but no one noticed us. I drove out on to the road with the utmost caution. I have always considered it essential to have complete assurance of the Lord's protection whenever I go into action in his name—but at the same time to take every possible precaution myself. God helps those who help themselves.

We returned by the same road. The sun was beginning to get lower in the sky.

'He has kept us on the second leg of our journey,' said my friend, seeing each stop no doubt as a fresh opportunity for the Lord to reveal his presence.

It was good to relax after the tension of each stop. We were tempted to get out of the car, go for a walk and just forget everything for a bit. But there was no time. As we neared our next rendezvous point, I felt a new tension, knowing the weight of our responsibility towards God. If we failed, effort and risks undertaken by others would be in vain.

Back on the open road we shook off our drowsiness by singing. We sang a great deal throughout the whole journey. What we sang came into our minds spontaneously, and always helped us. Without doubt it was God's doing, confirming his presence.

But little by little, fatigue was beginning to tell. We were crossing the mountains, and I could see that my friend was fighting the wheel at every hairpin bend.

'Let me take over now,' I offered.

'No,' he insisted. 'It is you who will be working tonight.'

Both of us fell silent. It was true; I had a lot to do that evening. People had been waiting for me for a long time, and I was sure to be immersed in discussions and questions until the small hours.

Another rendezvous point was near. It was odd, but

every fresh meeting seemed more difficult than the last. In this area particularly, meetings were hazardous. Cars were not common, and people's curiosity was quickly roused.

Again we were behind schedule as we looked for landmarks. We had been late everywhere—something I dislike. I began to give my friend instructions on how to get to the town centre.

The town was spread out over the hill like a fan. I was considering how best to stop, get out and go into the house where I was expected—all without being seen. There was no way that I could think of. 'Lord,' I murmured, 'please solve this problem for me.'

I wondered how he would do it. Perhaps he would make everyone stay indoors for a few minutes, or keep them away from the house I wanted to visit. Alternatively, he could just keep them from seeing, as he had done before.

As we drove into the town in a cloud of dust, the heavens opened. Rain poured down, and in a few moments the road was a mass of water. We stopped the car, because we couldn't see where we were going.

'Let's get everything ready,' I said, 'and I'll jump out while you carry on to the next street. Turn the corner and wait for me.'

The rain eased enough for us to go on, and as we approached the house I jumped from the car and hurtled into the courtyard. There was no one in the street at all: the rain was bucketing down. I reached the shelter of a projecting roof, then rushed through the door without pausing to knock.

There was a shout of surprise from a woman who was breast-feeding her child.

'Peace be with you, sister,' I greeted her, putting down my bag near the door. At this her face brightened. 'Please forgive me for not knocking,' I said, 'but I had to get into the house as quickly as possible.' I indicated the bag.

'May the Lord's peace be with you,' she said, still a bit uncertain.

'Is Brother B at home?'

She hesitated, glancing at the bag. 'Who are you?'

'A child of God.'

'Where are you from?'

'From the Lord's house.'

The woman smiled and stood up, leaving the child on a wooden bed. She opened the door into the next room, where a man of about fifty was lying. Brother B had obviously been listening to our conversation.

'He is rather ill,' said the woman.

'Ill?' I said. 'What's wrong?'

'It can't be helped,' said Brother B, with an effort. 'This body is so weak . . .'

Whenever I had seen him before he had always been full of energy, singing with great gusto and with a broad smile on his face. When he preached, it was impossible to remain unmoved.

'Get up, brother, and see what a treasure I've brought you,' I said lightly, not realising how ill he was.

'Well, if you say so—though I may be at death's door,' he replied. 'Guests like you don't come every day.'

Without realising what I was saying, I blurted out, 'I'm not telling you to get up. The Lord commands you to get up.' My voice sounded strange, and surprised me. I was shaking, and my lips were quivering. I don't know how I sounded to Brother B, but he leaped out of bed, still in his nightshirt, and embraced me warmly.

'You're dripping wet,' he said.

'Praise the Lord,' I replied. 'In the rain, no one can see anything.'

As he dressed I poured out all the Bibles on to his bed, and pushed them under his eiderdown.

'Oh,' he exclaimed, as the shirt fell from his fingers, 'how beautiful they are!' And as he turned the books over in his hands, he repeated, 'Lord, what a blessing you have brought into our house. Where are they from, brother? There is such a thirst for the Word of God here . . .'

I enjoyed watching as men like him savoured the pleasures of handling the Word of God. Such scenes show me the need, and encourage me to labour single mindedly for them, so that the spiritual famine can be satisfied.

Time, however, was not standing still. Already the sun was low on the horizon, and the shadows were lengthening. I would have to move on: I still had a lot to do that day.

'Please stay and have something to eat. Dry your clothes out a bit more,' he urged me.

'I haven't the time, brother. We have to go where the need is greatest.'

'But where isn't there a need? The few Bibles in our area are like a drop in the ocean. It's very difficult to distribute them under these conditions.'

'The Lord will help you,' I said. 'We shall be praying. But you haven't seen me or heard about me, all right? Neither you nor your wife.'

'Yes ... brother,' he agreed reluctantly, rather hurt that I had to go so soon. I said goodbye to them both and left the house in a hurry. The rain had stopped, and I could see the red sun struggling down towards the horizon. The air was clear. I walked with long strides, side-stepping the puddles.

Suddenly I heard quick footsteps behind me, and I turned. It was Brother B. Had I forgotten something? He signalled to me to wait, and soon drew level with me, panting for breath.

'Brother, do you know what? I've got no more pain—nothing. I'm cured!'

'Praise the Lord,' I said, and we stood there looking at each other for a moment. As we did so, someone came out of a nearby courtyard and looked us over very closely. I felt very uncomfortable. He passed us without saying anything. I thought for a minute, then went after him and stopped him.

'Do you have any idea where I could buy a bird?' I asked.

'Duck or chicken?' he replied, turning to me calmly.

'A turkey, if possible.'

'There are no more turkeys. Perhaps ... go a bit further, and ask again.'

'Thank you,' I said, and crossed the road. The man turned off to the left, and I did not see him again. When I returned to the car my friend was asleep, his head on the steering wheel. The fatigue and nervous strain had taken their toll. I felt bad about waking him, but I had little choice.

'Would you like me to take the wheel?' I offered again.

'No,' he replied sharply, and started the engine. Soon we were speeding along the wet asphalt road, but when we emerged from the town we found the road surface perfectly dry. The sun had disappeared behind the mountains ahead of us. I was tired, but my friend had recovered somewhat; the few moments of sleep had evidently done him good.

'Now to the fourth drop-off point,' he said. 'Jesus has been with us.' And he began to sing again.

By nightfall we would reach the next town, but I had no idea where the street we wanted was, apart from one or two vague memories. Asking a passer-by didn't seem advisable, and yet there were people waiting for me, and I had some important things to discuss with them. We had to find the way somehow.

Village after village went by, and the trees beside the road grew more thickly. It was getting really dark, and all the lights were on as we drove into town. I knew we had to cross the town centre and take a road on the right.

We ended up in a hollow, under the shadow of a hill. I got out of the car to try and spot some landmark, but I could not recognise anything. We were lost.

After thanking the Lord for bringing us to the town safely, we then asked him to help us find the street we wanted. My companion was rather annoyed that we had left without an address.

'What is the point of coming to the Lord now and asking him to lead you by the hand because you have forgotten the address or didn't bother to bring it?' he asked.

After we had prayed we were none the wiser—but I felt much calmer. My friend, however, was rather downcast.

I took the wheel and turned the car round. Without paying special attention or making a deliberate choice, I took the first street back into town. We drove along completely at random. I had no idea which way to go. All the time I was trying to recall the name of that street. I seemed to remember that it ended in 'sin', but that was all I could remember. Why hadn't I written it down? Perhaps, I thought, so that the Lord could demonstrate again that we could depend on him. I stopped the car.

'What shall we do now?' I asked.

'Wait,' said my companion.

'For what?'

'I don't know, brother. I don't know.' There was a trace of bitterness in his voice. Then he spoke again. 'There's someone coming. Ask him which street around here ends in "sin".'

I got out of the car. The man was drawing nearer and walking quickly. But he was so wrapped up in his own thoughts that he seemed oblivious to his surroundings. He noticed me only as he was about to pass me.

'Brother, I'm looking for a street . . .'

'Are you one of us then?' he interrupted, seizing on my use of the word 'brother'.

'Praise the Lord!' I exclaimed. 'He has sent you along to help us.'

I called out to my friend in the car; both of us were beside ourselves with joy—to the bewilderment of the man I had stopped. Dumbfounded, he looked at each of us in turn. At last his curiosity got the better of him.

'I don't understand, brothers . . .'

I wasn't sure how much to reveal, and hesitated. 'You see,' my friend stammered, 'we're looking for this street, but we don't know the name of it.'

'And how is that?' he asked, breaking into a laugh.

'We've forgotten,' continued my friend, 'but I'm sure you can tell us where Brother P lives . . .'

'Yes. It's not far from here.' And he tried to give us directions. But he spoke with a stutter, and we found it difficult to follow what he was saying. We looked at each other.

'Why don't you come with us in the car, and show us where he lives?' I suggested.

The man hesitated. He didn't really trust us. 'Who are you?' he asked.

'Brothers of yours. Brothers in Christ,' I replied.

'I see. You must be the men we're expecting. I was on my way to the meeting.'

He got in the car with us. My heart overflowed with joy and praise to God, and I could see that my companion had recovered his composure. When we stopped, our guide pointed towards a white house.

'Go in by the back door,' he said. 'I'll go and tell them at the church.'

The gate was wide open, as if guests were expected. At the end of a passage we emerged into a dimly lit courtyard. A light still shone in the window, and we knocked as directed. I waited, then knocked again, but there was no reply. We could hear voices, though, coming from inside; so I put my ear to the door and listened. Someone was praying. We didn't knock any more, but bowed our heads and prayed too, thanking the Lord that he had guided and protected us this far.

'Lord,' I heard a deeper and more powerful voice say, 'guide them in peace. Help them to get here as quickly as possible ...' Then the voice subsided. Heavy footsteps approached the door, and the key turned. Two powerful hands drew me inside.

'We were afraid something had happened to you,' said Brother P.

'No, praise the Lord. He has been with us. But we are late. Please forgive us.'

'You're here. That's the main thing.'

The house was clean and warm. It had the distinctive fragrance of true Christianity. But there was no time to stand and talk. We went to the car, I left what I had to leave for the Christians at that house, and we went on to the meeting.

'How are the Christians here?' I asked in the car.

'We are thankful to the Lord for everything,' said Brother P. 'When the sun shines we thank him that he has given us warmth; when it is cloudy we thank him that it is going to rain; and when there is a storm we thank him for the peace and calm that we know will follow.'

I sensed the difficulties they were facing. 'Yes,' I said, 'we have to give thanks for all things.'

'It's difficult,' he said. 'There are heavy fines to pay, for people who are as poor as church mice, for families with hordes of children. It's difficult. But every oppressor has an end. We thank the Lord that we can feel his coming is very near. Then we shall be delivered from all poverty, fines and mockery . . .'

I stopped the car some distance from the church, and the short walk had an invigorating effect. Brother P pushed open an old, high gate, and we entered another courtyard. Somewhere at the back a faint lamp was flickering. We walked gingerly along a very narrow, dark alley, and soon a large building loomed in front of us. It was high and long, and the roof looked strange in the half-light.

'You go first,' indicated Brother P, lifting the latch and opening the door into a passage. Everything was black with age. I could see a crowd of people gathered silently in a large room, all heads turned in our direction as they heard us.

The silence, broken momentarily as we entered, was quickly resumed. As we made our way to the front, the whole congregation stood up; then we all knelt down. A gentle murmur, like a soft evening wind, rose as they all thanked the Lord for seeing us safely to our destination. When we rose from our knees, Brother P spoke.

'We are delighted to welcome our brother into our midst. May the Lord bless him. Our brother can teach us a great deal. We will continue the service in meditation before the Lord as we listen to him.' And he motioned me towards the pulpit.

My heart was beating wildly. I was deeply moved, so that my eyes were soon full of tears. As I looked around, I could see that most of the congregation were young. Perhaps, I thought, they had been expecting someone younger . . .

I wasn't sure what to say, or how to begin. I was at the same time full and empty.

'Brothers,' I began, 'I beg you not to make us into more than we are. We are just your brothers in Christ—your servants for Christ's sake.' My eyes filled with tears again, and I felt a cold weight on my chest. I motioned to everyone to kneel, and we prayed together for a long time.

We rose from our knees again, tired but full of joy—a holy, heavenly joy that lightened our burdens and overwhelmed us. Then I addressed them again.

'It is a great joy to pass on greetings of your brothers in Christ from all over the country. They wish you much grace, peace and blessing from the Lord. They also desire that you make much progress in the Christian life for his glory.'

'Amen.' The response rippled round the room, and somewhere at the back there was a stir. A young man with a thick mop of hair rose to his feet, but someone hauled him down again.

'Say what you want to say, brother,' I called out. But he went red as a lobster, and remained silent.

'He wants to ask you,' said someone close to me, 'about . . .'

'Then let him ask,' I interrupted. 'Let him say what the Lord has put in his heart. We stand in his presence, and he knows the needs of each one of us.'

I had not prepared a sermon or chosen a text. I just had the Bible in front of me, and with it still closed I proposed to speak. Then an idea came into my mind.

'Brothers,' I said, thinking particularly of the young people, 'the Lord can lead you to ask something that is useful to us all. I think it would be good if we had some sort of sharing. Let's open our minds to the Word of God.'

I went down into the aisle. 'Let me hear your problems about the Scriptures, or about everyday life, and I will try to answer them, as the Lord enables. That way we can all learn. So, have you any problems?'

'Yes, brother.' A few voices from the right.

'Well, let's have them. Who has a question?'

There was silence. No one wanted to be first.

'In the Acts of the Apostles,' I said, 'a young man, described to us in a few words, had special qualities. He was full of the Holy Spirit and wisdom . . .'

'Stephen!' cried a woman.

With this, a series of questions was unleashed. Some odd, some interesting and some personal, they all reflected the concerns of the many young people there. And I could see that many of the problems were not understood by the older generation. Here, as everywhere, there were conflicts and misunderstandings between the two groups.

A schoolgirl asked how the Biblical version of creation related to what she had been taught; a boy questioned the value of books and films; a tall young man was worried about relationships between the sexes; many were interested in the Second Coming. In my replies I gave what I understood to be the biblical position, at the same time trying to break down barriers between old and young by explaining that they had much to give and teach each other.

There were many, many questions. Time was flying, but no one was in a hurry to return home. It seemed that I was expected to go on talking indefinitely. Suddenly a cock crowed in the courtyard outside, and there was much looking at watches and surprised shaking of heads. Brother P looked at me and saw that I was very tired.

'Brothers,' he said, 'I think that's enough for tonight. We are all like sponges—just absorbing—and our brothers are tired. They have taken a whole day to get here, and now they must leave. They have a long way to go today.'

2

The bridge crumbles

THE SILVERY rays of dawn filtered into the room, through the folds of the curtains, on to the wooden floor, the bed and my tired eyes. The day had been a heavy one, but I found it hard to go to sleep. Eventually I did, but after only about three hours an alarm clock shattered the silence, and my heavy eyelids had to open. I turned over, hoping to lie in a bit longer, but my host entered abruptly, a worried look on his face.

'I've had a very strange dream,' he said. 'Forgive me for troubling you, but I must tell you about it.'

'Please do,' I told him, rubbing the sleep from my eyes.

'It could be,' he began thoughtfully, 'that you were leaving, and I had gone out to show you the way. As I went out on to the main road, you were driving away, and I watched as you went into the distance, and were approaching a bridge. It didn't seem to be a proper bridge, just an improvised affair—something like a footbridge—and I was worried about the way you were driving. You seemed to be struggling with the steering wheel.

'Suddenly I could see that the bridge was beginning to split. The crack was getting wider and wider. I looked in turn at the car and the bridge, and shouted as loudly as I could for you to stop. You were too far away to hear; so I started running after you.

'I saw that something was going to happen, but how could I warn you? And how could something like that happen without the Lord knowing about it?'

'What happened after that?' I prompted.

'The crack in the bridge grew, and so did the danger that the whole structure would go crashing down into the ravine. As the car edged forwards, it seemed it would be on the bridge at the very second that everything collapsed. I shouted, "Step on it! Faster!" But you still didn't hear.

'I looked on in terror as the supports of the bridge began to give way, and I dashed forward in a futile effort to push your car across. At that moment the bridge split in two and started to sink. Then it collapsed with a loud crack. Your car seemed to rear up, hover in the air, and then disappear in an enormous cloud of dust.

'I fainted, and when I opened my eyes I was in bed—but still very frightened. I'm afraid something might happen to you. I didn't see anything more of you in the dream. The car vanished. All I could see was a pall of smoke and dust where the bridge had been.'

I tried to reassure him. 'Calm down, brother. We are going back the same way we came.'

'Yes, but who will help us?'

'The Lord has helped us so far.'

'But you will be in danger.'

'The Lord will take care of us,' I insisted. 'Anyway, my life has always been full of danger.'

Tiredness was beginning to tell on me. The little sleep we had had did not make things much easier. I felt dizzy, and my arms were heavy, but there was no time to waste. We had one more stop to make before the long drive home.

The sun was by now high in the sky; so I gathered my things together, checked the car and prepared to leave. My host saw me to the car, we embraced warmly, and he asked us to send him a postcard when we got back, to say that we had arrived safely. He stood watching as the car gathered speed.

The coolness of the morning, and the fact that we were on the last stage of our journey, encouraged us. I watched the countryside go past; hills, woods and rivers all seemed to be in harmony. The road was empty, and the car was going well.

'We'll soon be there,' I said to my friend at the wheel, giving him instructions as to how to approach the village and find the right address. He nodded, humming the same tune that he had been humming all day.

We entered the village, and he found the street with no trouble, parking the car skilfully in a tiny space. I left him near the car and, taking the packet with me, went off to look for the house. I recognised it, went up to the gateway, pulled aside the bolt and stopped as I went through. There was no one in the courtyard, or on the verandah.

When I tried the door opposite, it was locked, and the side door, too, I found shut. The man I had been expecting to see was obviously out, and I could not afford to wait for him. But I had to leave the packet there.

I circled the house again, but could find no suitable place to leave it. Then I noticed that one of the windows was slightly ajar, and succeeded in prising it open a little more—enough to slip the packet through. Then I thought for a moment, took out my thick pencil and wrote on the packet, 'From God to his children'. I pushed it through the window.

On my return to the car, my friend could see there was something wrong.

'Was there no one at home?' he asked.

'No one.'

'So what about the packet?'

'I pushed it through the window.'

'Well done,' he said. 'Praise the Lord!'

I motioned to him to change seats, and sat down behind the steering wheel. As we got under way, I added with a sigh, 'I would very much like to have spoken to that man.'

'Perhaps it was better that you didn't.'

'That's probably true.'

We emerged on to the main road—on our way home at last. From here it would be a non-stop drive. We started to sing again, but something seemed wrong. Something was not quite in order. Brother P's dream came back into my mind. Perhaps it was going to happen today, on this journey?

'What's up?' asked my friend.

'Oh, nothing.'

'You, Lord, are always with me,' he quoted, 'from the first to the last.' He emphasised the final words strongly.

The car was going downhill, and in front of us a wonderful view opened up—a little wood, a grove and a spring. As we went by I caught a sight of a secluded spot just off the road, and stopped. My friend looked at me questioningly.

'I want to pray before we go any further,' I said. So we bowed our heads, but I found it very hard. Something seemed to be hindering our prayers.

'Please pray,' I asked my friend, but he didn't seem in the right mood either. Both of us felt a weight—something hard to define. Eventually, though, he spoke, and his prayer grew bolder and bolder.

'I thank you, Lord, for having kept us on this journey until now. We commit the rest of it into your powerful hands. We belong to you, and we set out in your name. May your will be done.'

We drove off again. The sun had begun to sink, and the sky had turned greyish-blue. The road was fairly empty of traffic, but there were a number of people walking. We went on in silence, both of us wrapped up in our own thoughts. For some reason fear had begun to grip us. To try and relieve the tension, I began to sing, but my voice sounded strange and seemed to fizzle out somewhere in the area of the dashboard. I forced myself to continue. I would have liked to forget this road, everything—to shut my eyes for a moment and wake up in heaven, the country I longed for. A deep melancholy gripped me, as I looked sadly at the road stretching ahead.

As we came into a large village we could see from one end of it to the other along the wide street that bisected it. At the other end we caught sight of a man—a policeman—standing beside the road. I slowed down to well below the speed limit, and continued. He kept looking at us, and when we drew nearer he stared closely at the car, strode out into the middle of the road, gave a short blast on his whistle and flagged us down. I stopped as ordered—and wondered whether the dream was beginning to come true.

I got out of the car and walked towards the policeman. He saluted politely, but he wore a very serious expression and seemed slightly nervous as I handed him my papers.

'Where are you from?'

'I told him.

'And what brings you to this area?'

'I have some free time, and I can go where I want. That's why I bought the car. I wanted a rest. Apart from that, there are one or two problems I had to settle here.'

'What sort of problems?'

'Personal problems,' I replied. 'Everyone is allowed his problems, comrade.'

'What's your occupation?'

When I told him, he stared at me in amazement.

'Where do you work?'

'At the Ministry, comrade,' I replied in a slightly louder voice.

'I presume you're not on official business. So what are you doing here?'

'I'm free to travel, am I not?'

'It depends on your reasons. I've been waiting for you here for two days.'

'Really? Why is that? Haven't you other things to do?' I asked, growing a little bolder. Already I could feel the bridge cracking—but I knew I hadn't broken any traffic regulations, and there was no longer anything compromising in the car.

'It seems to me that you are here for other reasons, comrade,' he said in a milder tone, checking the number of the car again. 'I must ask you to come with me to the police station.'

I was about to go with him when he turned round as though he had forgotten something and began to rummage in the car. There was nothing for him to find, except my own New Testament. He showed me it.

'You're what they call an evangelical, aren't you?'

'Yes.'

'I thought my eyes weren't playing tricks. I knew I had the right car,' he said.

As we made our way to the police station I went over the journey in my mind, step by step, to try and see where they could have got on to my trail. But if he had been waiting two days . . .

It occurred to me that they might confiscate my car, but on reflection I hardly thought it likely, for I had nothing incriminating in it. However, I was afraid this affair might lead to complications that would hinder my work. The thought troubled me so much that it must have begun to show on my face, because when we entered the police station the officer remarked with a trace of irony and satisfaction in his voice, 'Not so cocky now, are we?'

'What's all the fuss about?' I asked, plucking up courage again. 'I haven't murdered anyone, have I?'

'We didn't say you'd murdered anyone.'

'Well, let me go, then. I'm in a hurry. Tomorrow I've got to be back at the Ministry.' I stressed the last word.

'Not so fast. You don't tell us what to do.'

I fell discreetly silent.

'Where did you say you were from?'

'I've already told you. I'm just out for a run in the car.'

'Stop beating about the bush. You're an intelligent man, and here you are wasting your time with things of no value.'

'I do what I like with my free time, just as you do.'

'The mere mention of the world "evangelical" is enough to make me squirm—though there aren't any of your sort around here.'

'There is much that makes them squirm as well,' I retorted, 'especially when they hear about certain other sorts of people. But at least they continue to mind their own business.'

The policeman glowered at me. But he saw he wasn't getting anywhere; so he took my papers and crossed the road to the town hall. After a few moments he emerged, accompanied by a short, fat man. They stopped to look at my car, and appeared to be discussing something. Then they came and asked me to go with them into another room, and all three of us sat down around what appeared to be a conference table.

'Comrade mayor,' said the policeman, introducing me to the stout man. 'He wants to know why you have been travelling around these parts.'

'Today is a Sunday, comrade, and I am as free as you are to go where I wish and do what I want.'

'But not to contravene the laws of the state,' interrupted the mayor.

'I am not aware of having broken any law. But if I have, tell me which one.'

'You may think not, but we haven't been waiting for you here for nothing. I received orders from my superiors not to let you pass. We cannot have people like you roaming around visiting evangelicals, giving sermons, bringing Bibles ... and I don't know what else ...' He turned to the policeman. 'These evangelicals are an absolute plague. They go around the countryside organising meetings where they talk to people about repentance, speak against the state and twist men's minds.'

'In which villages did you preach?' the policeman asked me.

'In none.'

'Tell the truth.'

'I have.'

'You are among the most embittered people against the state. Show us your preacher's licence!'

'I haven't got one.'

'There you are: you've broken the law. Don't you know that in this country no one has the right to preach unless he obtains permission? Don't you know that the state appoints and recognises only preachers who are loyal?'

'You can't prove that I have preached anywhere,' I replied. 'And I haven't broken any of your laws.'

They looked at each other.

'What are you trying to tell us? Are you trying to teach us the law? Do you think we're going to stand for this?

The party has given us authority. You're against the party and against the state.'

The policeman leafed through the papers again. The mayor took a piece of paper and began to write down details, spelling each word out syllable by syllable as he did so. Then he looked at the policeman, read out everything he had written and handed me back my papers.

'This information will be of use to us, and if it transpires that you have been to any secret meetings, been preaching anywhere or otherwise distorting men's minds, we shall be able to find you without any difficulty,' he said.

'That's your worry,' I told him, taking back my papers and rising to leave.

As I reached the door, I turned to the two men, who were still sitting at the table, and said, 'Perhaps you will now be good enough to tell me why you have kept me here, and wasted so much of my time. I demand to know the reason.'

They looked at each other in blank amazement. Then the mayor rushed up to me.

'Are you looking for trouble?'

'I demand an answer.'

'Very well. It was for going around with contraband, disguised as an evangelical.'

'What contraband?'

'Are you pretending you don't know? Do you think the alarm was raised for no reason?'

I pushed the door open. 'Contraband? What a suggestion!' I exclaimed, and made for the car.

The sun was sinking fast, the shadows of the trees spreading right across the road. My friend, who had been praying all the time, was waiting impatiently in the car.

'They think we're smugglers!' I said, turning the ignition key.

The car gathered speed as the sun merged with the grey horizon. It was a strange, untimely sunset. Both earth and sky seemed plunged into sorrow.

The following day I received a postcard. In large, rounded letters the message read, 'The bridge is cracking, and the supports have been shaken.'

We had emerged unscathed, but I knew where this first setback would very quickly and easily lead. For the moment, at least, there could be no more travelling in Bibles.

Some other titles in Lakeland Paperbacks

YOUNG CHRISTIANS IN RUSSIA
Michael Bourdeaux and Katharine Murray
Based on authentic documents and reports from inside the Soviet Union, here is exciting evidence of the growth of Christian faith among the younger generation.

CZECH MATE   *David Hathaway*
Over the years a British pastor took 150,000 Bibles and Testaments behind the Iron Curtain. Then he was imprisoned in Czechoslovakia.

FORGIVE ME, NATASHA   *Sergei Kourdakov*
A young Russian police officer's own story of his brutal persecution of Christians, and of his search for their God.

I FOUND GOD IN SOVIET RUSSIA   *John Noble*
Through the witness of his fellow prisoners in Soviet labour camps the author, an American citizen, was brought to belief in Christ.

TORTURED FOR HIS FAITH   *Haralan Popov*
The stirring testimony of a Bulgarian pastor, imprisoned for thirteen years for preaching the Christian gospel.